Praise for Rogue L

C000010275

With all of the challenges facing schools tod~~ay, it's more important~~ than ever for educators to keep learning, growing, and adapting. In *ROGUE Leader*, Rich Czyz presents even more fantastic ideas and resources for making professional development meaningful and engaging. You'll find creative strategies you can use right away to build new knowledge.

—Dr. David Geurin, author of *Future Driven: Will Your Students Thrive in an Unpredictable World?*

We have all fallen victim to irrelevant, meaningless, one-and-done professional development. *ROGUE Leader* is a must-read for leaders who want explicit guidance about how to create differentiated, purposeful professional development and engage teachers and staff members in unconventional ways. Rich has done it again!

—Pamela Hernandez, NJ Visionary Principal of the Year 2019

Rich Czyz shares his wisdom, humor, and experiences, cleverly designed as the blueprint for you to take control of your own PD destiny. Czyz writes in a masterful way that will inspire you to create a meaningful change in your professional learning by going ROGUE and charting your own course.

—Barbara Bray, speaker, podcast host, and author of *Define Your Why*

Czyz provides a roadmap for educators to design their learning journey and supports educators through encouragement, inspiration and prompts for reflection that will empower them to make meaningful changes in their teaching practice today.

—Rachelle Dené Poth, educator, author, consultant, attorney

The message throughout *ROGUE Leader* is that professional development is personal and should provide the means to benefit students by making us better educators. This book will serve as a great how-to for leaders in education concerned about appropriate and relevant professional development.

—Michael G Curran Jr., EdD, professor emeritus, Rider University

This book is packed full of useful and relevant activities for teachers leading or attending professional development. What teacher who cares about the professional development of other teachers wouldn't want to read this?

—**Joyce Matthews FRSA,** award-winning facilitator, International Association of Facilitators

This book is great for both teachers and administrators. Rich Czyz makes me reflect on how I can help my staff to continue to grow. There are so many examples of what good PD can look like, and I'm definitely inspired to be better.

—**Jay Billy,** author of *Lead with Culture: What Really Matters in Our Schools*

Rich Czyz provides a new vision for sincere and meaningful professional development. This book will mentor any leader who wants to provide relevant and meaningful learning experiences for all educators.

—**Sean Gaillard,** author of *#ThePepperEffect*

I have been a huge fan of Rich Czyz and his work for years. As a leader, you will walk away from his book inspired, pumped, and ready to make a meaningful change to professional development in your setting.

—**Dr. Rachael George,** coauthor of *She Leads*

Do you long for harmony, connection, and meaning in PD? Do you want a vibrant school culture that nurtures learning and resilience? Read *Rogue Leader* for fresh perspectives on PD and actionable ideas to guide you!

—**Laura Gilchrist,** vice-president of ParentCamp

Rogue Leader

Take Control of Your Own
PD Destiny!

Thanks for being a
ROGUE Leader!

R. SB

ROGUE
Leader

Make the Rules,
Inspire Others, and
Take Control
of Your Own
Professional
Development
Destiny

Rich Czyz

Rogue Leader: Make the Rules, Inspire Others, and Take Control of Your Own Professional Development Destiny
© 2022 Rich Czyz

All rights reserved. No part of this publication may be reproduced in any form or by any electronic or mechanical means, including information storage and retrieval systems, without permission in writing by the publisher, except by a reviewer who may quote brief passages in a review. For information regarding permission, contact the publisher at books@daveburgessconsulting.com.

This book is available at special discounts when purchased in quantity for educational purposes or for use as premiums, promotions, or fundraisers. For inquiries and details, contact the publisher at books@daveburgessconsulting.com.

Published by Dave Burgess Consulting, Inc.
San Diego, CA
DaveBurgessConsulting.com

Library of Congress Control Number: 2021953181
Paperback ISBN: 978-1-956306-09-5
Ebook ISBN: 978-1-956306-10-1

Cover and interior design by Liz Schreiter
Edited and produced by Reading List Editorial
ReadingListEditorial.com

*To the four people who are always
in my corner:
Megan, Meredith, Olivia, and Malcolm.*

*You support me every step of the way.
You inspire me each day to be a better
husband, father, educator, and writer.
You mean everything to me.*

Contents

Introduction

The Road Behind and the Road Ahead

W hen I started this journey several years ago, I recognized that the professional development (PD) systems in many of our schools were broken. My experiences demonstrated that those in charge were limited in being able to provide meaningful and relevant PD to individual educators. I saw a lot of one-size-fits-all, one-and-done, whole-group sessions that didn't help many teachers grow as professionals. As a novice teacher, I didn't know any better. I assumed that someone else would be responsible for my professional growth and keep my best interests in mind. But as I grew as a teacher and learner myself, I knew that there had to be a better way for professional development to be organized and delivered. A few years later, I became an administrator in charge of professional development, and I vowed that I would not let teachers have the same experience that I had. I found that I couldn't possibly know or plan the kind of PD that would help every educator in the room. In order for teachers to get exactly what they needed, they had to be involved in the decision-making process surrounding PD. From that moment on, I tried to empower other educators to take charge of their own professional development.

What I learned in those years, first as a teacher and then as an administrator, helped me to write my PD manifesto, *The Four O'Clock*

Faculty: A Rogue Guide to Revolutionizing Professional Development, to help schools and districts improve their PD practices to make it more meaningful and relevant for *all* educators. As I stated in that book:

Pursuing learning and professional development is the single most important action we can take to hone our craft as educators.

Several years later, this statement still holds weight. There is nothing more important we can do to improve as educators than to take charge of our own professional development destiny. Before we move forward in figuring out exactly how to do that, it's important that you have an understanding of the ideas presented in *The Four O'Clock Faculty*. In case you haven't gotten to read it yet, here's a quick review of what I covered in the previous book.

My Core Beliefs on PD

As a planner of professional development for many years, I have come to form several beliefs about professional learning and what it needs to include in order to be successful. The following tenets should guide any planning of professional development activities:

- Professional learning should be meaningful and relevant to an educator's role.
- Educators should have some choice in what they learn and how they learn it.
- Professional development time is precious. It should never be wasted on meaningless activities.

- One-way communication, like lists of policies, bulleted items, and reminders, should be emailed to staff members, *not* read to them.
- Professional development must focus on improving learning outcomes for students and teachers.
- Your professional learning is the responsibility of only one person: *you.*

The Role of Choice in PD

Choice matters in professional development. Looking back at the number of PD sessions I have attended over the years, I see that I was much more likely to buy in to a topic that I was engaged in versus being forced to sit through a session that didn't meet my needs. Just as choice helps students to become more engaged in the learning process, choice for teachers can support engagement in professional learning. Providing a wide variety of workshops and learning formats and the freedom to choose their own path for learning helps to ensure teachers receive information and resources that are relevant to their students, classrooms, needs, and interests.

What Does It Mean to Go ROGUE?

If you are not getting what you need in terms of professional development, sometimes you need to go ROGUE and chart your own course to make professional learning happen for you and others around you. R-O-G-U-E, as defined in the first book, is a Relevant Organized Group of Underground Educators. You will see this term throughout this book as well. You need to understand that ROGUE educators push their own professional learning boundaries. They find other committed, dedicated learners who are willing to collaborate and share. They are interested in the cause of making PD more meaningful. ROGUE educators understand that they may have to do things on their own in order to get what they need.

Connecting with Others

There are many experts out there waiting to collaborate and share. If you are not finding what you need in terms of professional development in your school or setting, you can reach out to connect with others around the world. Connecting with others via social media apps like Twitter or Voxer can help you to learn from experts outside of your physical proximity. If you are the only teacher at your grade level or are in the unique position of being the only content specialist in your school, it can be difficult to share and bounce ideas off of others. Many educators use social media to find others who are interested in redefining professional development. Educators can now learn anytime, anywhere, and connect with professional learning communities outside their own schools to continuously grow as professionals. In fact, you'll learn more about the #4OCFPLN, an online professional learning community that grew out of a book study on *The Four O'Clock Faculty*, later in this book.

Dealing with Disappointing PD

The truth is, no matter how much effort we put into improving PD, all educators will face bad professional development experiences at some point in their career. You will need to remember that in most cases, you will have no control over bad PD. You can only control how you react to it. There are several options you can employ when dealing with disappointing PD. Tune out and learn nothing. Sit, listen, and hopefully learn something. Use the time to get something done, like finding and sharing resources. Ask questions in order to find out specifics and engage in critical thinking about the session topic. Speak up and challenge the presenter or facilitator. This one might feel the best in the moment, but it can be tricky to pull off respectfully. Ultimately, if you are not getting what you need, exercise your free choice and find something that will contribute to your learning. Get up and leave. Go online. Talk to a colleague. Find something to do to be productive instead of sitting through PD that isn't helpful to you!

PDIY

There is only one way to do professional development if you want it done right. Do it yourself. Turn the DIY movement into the PDIY movement—Professionally Develop It Yourself. Let's continue to expand our definition of professional learning, giving ourselves more choices and options, incorporating various learning styles, modeling the types of learning that should be happening with our students, and providing continuous learning so that everyone's education achieves the depth it deserves. For professional development to be effective, it must be designed to engage educators on relevant and meaningful topics. Ultimately, it must help transform practices in the classroom, giving teachers the tools to develop their craft and practice.

Now that you have a basic understanding of some of the ideas brought forward in *The Four O'Clock Faculty*, we are ready to look to the road ahead and continue to create PD to inspire and innovate! You can also visit the #4OCF website to find more information and additional book resources from *The Four O'Clock Faculty*, such as MicroLearning videos, #PopUpPD resources, and other professional development strategies:

Since the first book came out, I have spent time in several schools and among educators proselytizing about PD as the single most important action we can take to hone our craft. I have spoken with many educators—teachers and administrators alike—who still experience struggles related to professional development. During this time, I myself have continued to learn and grow as an educator. I have learned that there is still work to be done, and the most beautiful thing about our PD systems is that they can constantly grow, evolve, and improve to help all educators. I state this with one caveat: our PD systems have the ability to grow and evolve when all of us are invested in improving the systems. It takes a great deal of work by everyone to ensure that PD is done right—administrators, teachers, and even students can take responsibility to provide meaningful and relevant professional development.

I want to take this opportunity to share some of the additional things I've learned in my constant journey to improve PD. One of the best parts of writing about innovating in the professional development space is that others have been inspired to innovate and share their best PD practices. I've been able to share with, collaborate with, and learn from those who are in the field working to improve professional development—the ROGUE Leaders putting in the work.

In the coming pages, you will find:

- More professional development strategies and practices to make all of us better,
- Answers to some of the burning questions that have been asked since the first ROGUE guide came out,
- PD Rules before each chapter that will help make professional development the best that it can possibly be,
- PD Checkpoints at the end of each chapter that provide activities to try right away to help you to clarify your core beliefs about professional development, and
- Planning ideas for the three stages of PD: the beginning, the middle, and the end, where you will find strategies to

effectively engage educators in meaningful PD that may often be overlooked.

Simply put, I want you to walk away from this book inspired to create a meaningful change in your professional development practice. I want you to become a ROGUE Leader in your own right, someone who can improve our professional development system incrementally. By doing so, we can all lift our PD systems to newfound heights and push ourselves forward as educators.

When you joined the Four O'Clock Faculty in the first place, you knew there was work to be done. You knew it might be an uphill battle, but you were willing to take the risk to shift the PD paradigm. You may have started to move the needle and improve professional development for yourself and some of your colleagues. Guess what? There is still more that can be done. We need to begin to move everyone along with us.

It's time, once again.

ROGUE Leaders unite.

Make the rules. Inspire others. Take control of your own PD destiny.

The journey isn't over. It's only just beginning.

It's time for the ROGUE encore.

Who's with me?

PD Rule: Always Meet with a Purpose

Let's begin with the idea of rules. We put rules in place to assume some kind of order out of chaos. Many people like rules because they do provide structure and organization. Many others will push back against rules, knowing that they are sometimes meant to be broken. I stand somewhere planted firmly in the middle. PD rules give us an opportunity to define what will improve our professional learning processes. Simply put, they allow us to plan PD that works.

Let's start with Rule #1:
Always meet with a purpose

It seems obvious, but in many of our schools and districts, there are PD gatherings held regularly because they need to be scheduled. Many of those in charge of PD assume that if professional development sessions are planned and held, teachers will learn. This is the seat-time theory of PD. If we put educators in seats, they will learn, right? There may be no thought put into the purpose of why you are actually bringing those educators together in the first place.

Too many times, our PD is the result of thoughtlessness. Someone realizes that there is a PD session coming up next week and quickly throws together a half-baked plan to fill the time. There is no intentionality behind the plan, and it comes across in the delivery of the session. People realize that they are just adding to the checklist. One more thing checked off, and teacher seat time is documented. Professional development, done and checked off.

We all know that this shouldn't be the case. PD should be carefully planned and considered. Each staff member's unique needs should be examined before putting forth a plan.

In her book *The Art of Gathering: How We Meet and Why It Matters*, Priya Parker outlines the importance of purpose. She recognizes that planners of all kinds of gatherings—business meetings, parties, social events, even casual hangouts—most likely miss the most important part.

Parker states, "You are not alone if you skip the first step in convening people meaningfully: committing to a bold, sharp purpose."

In education, bold, sharp purpose in PD often takes a back seat to other things—timing, logistics, resources, and mandates. Instead of focusing on all of these tangential planning pieces, we need to focus on why we are meeting in the first place.

So, PD rule #1: always meet with a purpose.

Decide your "why" before you schedule that staff meeting. Just because it's scheduled on a calendar doesn't mean you need to have it. Understand the direction and focus of your district-wide PD event before you gather everybody in one large room and talk at them.

Professional development with a purpose. How novel!

Be intentional. Meet with a purpose in mind. Share that purpose with everyone involved. Let them know why you are gathering. Give them a reason for being there.

Defining your purpose will ultimately improve your PD sessions.

Chapter 1

The Dirty Word

"Only I didn't say 'fudge.' I said *the* word, the big one, the queen mother of dirty words, the 'F-dash-dash-dash' word."

—RALPHIE IN *A CHRISTMAS STORY*

When I started my teaching career, I was young and naive. I loved opportunities for professional development in those early years—both those within my own building and district and those outside the district. As a young teacher, I was constantly looking to grow through PD opportunities, so I was constantly on the lookout for interesting sessions where I thought I could grow and bring something back to my students. Because of my naivete, I thought every one of my colleagues felt the same way. I quickly realized, however, that not everyone was as enthusiastic about PD as I was.

I found that others despised professional development. I just didn't see it. What is it about professional development that sucks? Why do people hate it so much? Why does it deserve such a poor reputation?

Throughout most of my career, and even as I began the ROGUE journey several years ago, the term itself has been a dirty word in education. Just like Ralphie saying the wrong thing in *A Christmas Story*, utter the term "professional development" and risk having your mouth rinsed out with soap.

I think mostly it's about time. No one wants to waste their precious time. Especially teachers. They could be doing something else worthwhile. Something more meaningful. Something more relevant to their jobs.

But instead, here they are. Sitting. Watching. Listening (or not). Grading papers. Checking email. Counting the number of ceiling tiles. Finding any excuse to zone out. Wishing they could just be somewhere else.

And somehow it still continues. PD is still hit-or-miss. It falls along a large continuum. PD can be great or it can be really terrible.

Professional development. The phrase for many still conjures negativity, pessimism, and defeat. Teachers are ready to run for the hills or, at the very least, take the day off instead of attending. All this time, it has made me wonder: Are we too far gone with professional development? Can we ever fully recover or will professional development always have such a negative connotation in education?

It took me a few years, but I came to an important realization. My professional development was going to be my responsibility alone.

A few years ago, I thought I was on the right path. I thought I knew how to fix the problems of professional development. I advocated for everyone to take responsibility for their own learning path. If everyone did this, then the world would be a beautiful place (at least in terms of PD).

Call it "PDtopia." Or maybe "Perfection PD." Perhaps "the Land of Milk and Honey (and PD)."

Birds chirp.

A teacher walks to a professional development session of their own choosing happily conversing with a colleague.

A choir sings.

Smiles and laughter abound as educators move to and fro, learning exactly what they need to grow as teachers and individuals.

In PDtopia, everything is aligned with school and district goals, and more importantly, student outcomes.

I know that it can exist. PDtopia. The happiest place on earth.

Except . . .

What we end up with is a more realistic setting that might be better known as PD purgatory.

The stench of stale air and old books overwhelms the tiny library where the large staff almost causes the room to burst at the seams.

Everyone talks about anything other than the topic, and everyone wishes they were anywhere else.

Expressions of miserable fatigue dot the room.

The presenter, who was brought in from outside the district, reads from a "timeless" slide presentation. (And by "timeless," I mean "terribly dated.")

He, of expert status, tells you how you should be teaching, as if he knows anything about the individual students you work with or their specific needs. While he reads to you, directly from the slides, you realize that this is the same presentation that you saw just two years ago. Word for word.

Oh, professional development. Will it always be a dirty word? Will it always be this bad?

It doesn't have to be, but it will take effort to make a difference.

How do we change it? How do we stop professional development from being the mother of all dirty words associated with education? ("Oh, fudge!!!")

It starts with bringing some respect and prestige back to the phrase. The term itself dates to the 1800s but came into wide usage in the 1960s. When educators began using it, I don't think they were bristling with displeasure, discontent, and disapproval. The reputation was earned over the years built upon *bad* PD. The key to turning around the reputation of professional development lies in delivering outstanding PD sessions.

Why do you focus on the phrase professional development instead of professional learning?

I was asked this question repeatedly after releasing the original ROGUE guide. People wanted to know why I used the phrase "professional development." Many pointed out that the phrase has such a negative connotation in education that it might be better to phrase it differently so that teachers take a different approach to professional development.

I would tend to agree.

We have arrived at the point where the two words, when uttered together, have come to exist in a very negative space in education. Many educators cringe when they hear the words. Most educators have a negative experience associated with professional development.

Many have done exactly what was suggested to me and tried to change the phrase in order to improve the connotation.

Professional learning, professional growth, teacher development, staff in-service, etc.

Bad PD under any other name is just bad PD. If you host a "professional growth" day and still make the same mistakes by delivering one-size-fits-all solutions, you will eventually tarnish the term "professional growth."

The key is making sure that whatever term you use is backed by meaningful learning for teachers. If it has an impact, it won't matter what you call it.

In order to change the connotation of the words, start with a few steps:

1. *Admit the mistakes that have taken place.* A simple acknowledgment of the problem will go a long way in starting down the road of changing the perception of PD. Admit to colleagues: "I know that PD hasn't been what it should be, and I'm committed to making it purposeful." Admitting that there is a problem with professional development in the first place will allow you to look at it with a different lens.

2. *Outline the reasons why it's been problematic.* Once you see the problems that exist within your professional development system, you can begin to shift your plans to overcome those mistakes. Determine the struggle points within professional development. Write down all of the reasons why it doesn't work as currently constituted. Creating this list might be painful but it will help you to eventually plan more meaningful professional development.

3. *Commit to a new definition of the term.* Now that you've defined everything that made the term a dirty word for you and your colleagues, create a new definition. You can begin with a sentence starter, like "Professional development in my school (or district) is..." or "Quality professional development must have..." Your new definition of the word can then be shared with everyone so they understand what PD could and should be. Think of this as your PD mission statement. What do we want PD to be?

4. *Define the words through action.* This is the most important part. Once you have your mission statement for PD, you need to make sure that every session defines the words through action. You can't say that teacher choice is a huge part of professional development but then only offer it sometimes. Each PD offering needs to come back to the words shared in the definition. If you allow any of those struggle points or problematic

areas to creep into even just one session, the educators around you will realize that it's the same old PD as usual. Don't allow the past practices to sabotage your ability to deliver powerful, effective professional development.

In the next chapter, you will find specific questions you can ask to ensure that you are thinking about professional development in the proper context. The questions will help you to determine readiness for a PD system that works to meet both individual goals and needs, while balancing the overall needs of all educators within the system (whether at the school or district level). No matter your role in planning or delivering professional development, you can be a ROGUE Leader by understanding a few basic tenets about PD.

It's time that we reclaim the term "professional development." We don't need to think of it as a dirty word in education. We don't need to hide behind or create euphemisms for PD. It can be powerful, purposeful, and consequential. We just have to put in the effort to make it happen.

ROGUE Leader Reflections

PD Keys

☞ Professional development does *not* need to be a dirty word in education. In order for educators' opinions to change, you must build a reputation based on top-notch PD offerings.

☞ Outline the reasons why you think professional development is a dirty word amongst your colleagues. Explore the why behind what makes people hate PD.

☞ Commit to a new definition of the term professional development. Back up the new definition with consistent action.

A Question to Ponder

What values, attributes, and characteristics do you want to associate with quality professional development?

After each chapter in the book, you will see a PD Checkpoint. This will be a brief, fun activity that will ask you to think about a certain aspect of professional development. Take a few moments to read through the checkpoint and answer any questions or complete any activities that are included. Hopefully the checkpoints will help you think about how you can begin to improve PD in your own setting.

Here we go!

PD Checkpoint #1: It Was Professor Plum with the PD in the Study!

The object of the board game Clue is to use your deductive reasoning skills to determine who committed the murder at the center of the game! As a top-notch detective, you can use the process of elimination to determine what type of weapon Professor Plum used to murder Mr. Boddy (or Dr. Black, if you're playing Cluedo)!

Use the process of elimination to determine the best type of PD for you! Cross out PD characteristics that don't work for you:

Solo	Collaborative	Active Listening	Interactive
Creating	Building/Making	Hands-On	Discussion-Based
Small Group	Large Group	Job-Embedded	Teacher-Driven
Student-Led	Active Participation	Ongoing	Data-Based
Practical	Intensive	Reflective	Goal-Oriented
Models Lessons	Personalized	Inquiry-Based	Mentoring
Coaching	Content-Focused	Expert Support	Offers Feedback

Now that you've eliminated some choices, circle three options that work well for you! Write down an idea for a PD session that features all three of the characteristics you chose.

PD Rule #2: Be Consistent

It can be hard to try to anticipate everyone's needs. It can be difficult to motivate colleagues if they've had bad PD experiences. Trying to cram everything into an hour-long PD session is often easier said than done. In addition, the lack of time for professional development often derails it before we can even begin.

Many PD planners struggle with the burdensome and challenging nature of delivering quality professional development. It often gets placed on the back burner in favor of easier tasks and initiatives. One of the reasons that professional development is often not successful is the lack of consistency.

A PD day might be planned and delivered at the beginning of the year before students start back for the year. A new initiative will be introduced, and teachers will receive some training for a couple of hours. Teachers may not see additional training on that new initiative until sometime in the middle of the school year. At that time, they haven't given any thought to the opening PD in four to six months.

Inconsistent delivery of PD will stop motivation and momentum dead in its tracks.

So, rule #2: be consistent.

Make PD a regular part of the routine. If you are focusing on a school-wide goal for the year, dedicate several minutes to it at each monthly staff meeting. Meet weekly with colleagues to discuss what's working or not working in the classroom. Find a consistent time that can be dedicated to professional learning.

When I was a kid, my school used to have half-day dismissals once a month. I loved it because I used to get to go out to lunch with my family instead of eating lunch in the cafeteria. What I never realized, though, was that the school used the time each month for instructional planning purposes and professional development opportunities. It was a consistent session each month when the teachers were able to come together to collaborate and learn from each other.

While scheduling half-day sessions may not be a possibility at your school, the opportunity for consistency is still there. Required staff meetings should include some PD each month. Teacher mastermind groups can meet each week. Daily conversations with grade-level partners and department colleagues can help push everyone toward growth.

Be consistent. Find the time that is available. Don't skip out on an opportunity to grow and learn. Professional development should be a priority all year long, not just when it is convenient within the schedule. Small consistent practices can lead to big long-term results.

Don't let school get in the way of learning. Be consistent in your practice and in your own professional growth.

Chapter 2

Are you READI?

> "Too many professional development initiatives are done to teachers—not for, with, or by them."
>
> —Andy Hargreaves

As I've spoken with educators who are interested in shifting their own PD paradigms, one of the frequent questions I've been asked is, "How do I design PD that works?" As I've thought more and more about this, I've realized that there is not one type of professional development that will meet everyone's needs.

It almost becomes like a PD version of "Goldilocks and the Three Bears."

This PD is too hot. This PD is too cold.

This PD is too short. This PD is too long.

This PD is too interactive. This PD is not interactive enough.

It seems that no matter what type of PD is planned, you may not be able to meet the needs of everyone involved. So instead of thinking about planning the *perfect* PD session or day, you need to think about the overall goals you have for professional development.

I've designed the READI framework to help professional development planners and ROGUE Leaders ensure that they are planning PD that meets a number of different goals related to both individual educators and school and district goals. You need to consider how a PD session fits into your overall goals for professional development. While you can't plan the perfect PD offerings to meet *all* demands, you can organize PD in such a way that educators find it relevant and meaningful, and you still deliver the content colleagues need while addressing district and school goals.

The READI framework provides five areas to consider as you plan:

- Relevance
- Embeddedness
- Alignment
- Design
- Impact

Let's look at each area more closely.

READI Framework: Relevance

One of the major issues with most PD sessions is the lack of relevance for educators. An eighth-grade ELA teacher must attend a guided math workshop? The new kindergarten teacher must attend a session on state testing strategies? When planning PD, we simply need to do better. We've mentioned the problem with the one-size-fits-all approach.

Even in schools or districts where a one-size-fits-most plan is utilized, teachers are still shuffled in and out of sessions that may be only loosely tied to their content or area of expertise. It becomes an exercise in futility. Teachers are left to feel befuddled, bewildered, and baffled by the PD planning process. "Why am I being asked to attend this session? It has nothing to do with what I teach!" becomes an all too common refrain.

Relevance is a difficult ask because of the varied positions, content areas, subjects, experiences, and expertise that each of us brings to the table. For PD planners, it is incredibly difficult to ensure that everyone is getting exactly what they want or need. The elementary music teacher has different needs compared to the secondary school nurse. Even within an individual department, the first-year biology teacher has very different needs than the thirty-year veteran teaching physical science.

The days of one PD workshop that every educator attends need to be long gone. We can't move forward with a one-size-fits-all mindset. We need to consider application for every educator. Does the session that we ask an educator to attend have anything to do with their role or expertise? Loosely based should be not an acceptable criteria. Relevance needs to lead to impact. How far are we asking an educator to stretch themselves in attending a session outside their content area? While it is sometimes necessary to ask teachers to participate in session completely outside their area of expertise, we need to be careful that the learning taking place will be applicable in the classroom.

Starting Point: Is this PD session relevant to what educators do each day?

If your answer is yes, then you've done a great job planning. If the answer is no, then you have a little bit of work to do.

Use surveys and teacher feedback: Gain insight into teacher perspective by conducting a survey or asking for teacher feedback about professional development. Asking a few simple questions about preferences, wants, and needs can provide valuable information to guide planning. Use a free online survey tool like SurveyMonkey or Google Forms to ask a few basic questions that will get at teacher attitudes, desires, and needs for professional learning. Once you have the feedback, use it to help plan relevant sessions for everyone involved.

Provide teacher choice and multiple pathways: After gathering data from surveys, use your planning process to arrange sessions that cover a number of relevant areas. General topics that might apply across grade levels and subject areas can be included to provide options for teachers who might not need specific content workshops. Discussions about assessment, classroom design, and restorative practices can apply to a variety of educators and provide interesting content options. Offer a variety of different types of sessions as well. Discussions, interactive presentations, modeled lessons, collaborative work sessions, creative jam sessions, problem-solving summits, and more can help engage colleagues in different ways. Give careful consideration to whether the PD opportunities offered give teachers true choice—a variety of session topics, formats, and planned outcomes. Will teachers find something that works for them and helps their students with what they teach?

READI Framework: Embeddedness

It is always difficult to implement a new instructional strategy or worthwhile program when you get back from a good PD session. How many times have you gone to a PD session and felt like you would like to implement the idea but don't have the time or support to make it happen? PD stumbles occur regularly—one-and-done sessions with no further explanation or chance to ask questions after implementation. Start and stop becomes your reality. This will probably be the only time that you will receive training on this new concept. You may not have time within your schedule for implementation. You may have other mandated lessons that take precedence. You may not have any additional support in implementing the new strategy. No one is there in the classroom after the workshop to help you work through the implementation. But it doesn't have to be this way.

So much of our professional learning is only surface-level. In and out. No chance to really delve headfirst into a topic, or to try, fail, and try again in the classroom. Educators need to practice implementation with plenty of time and support. They need to be able to ask questions, to troubleshoot with someone, to collaborate and adapt while changing their classroom practices. Professional learning needs to be embedded in classroom practices after the initial learning takes place. Strong PD is already deeply rooted in what teachers do each day. It gives them the chance to learn about a topic in order to change and build on existing classroom practices.

Starting Point: Is this PD session embedded in what educators do?

If the answer is yes, then you've spent some time prioritizing school or district PD goals and what teachers actually need while making sure professional learning is implemented and embedded in classrooms. If the answer is no, you may need to consider some of the following options:

Instructional coaching: PD needs to be directly embedded in the classrooms if the ultimate goal of professional development is improved student learning outcomes. PD that is entrenched in teacher work typically happens within the school day, and often includes students in the classroom. The perfect opportunity to embed professional development during the school day is by using instructional coaching. I've had the opportunity to implement and benefit from coaching in the past, and it's truly one of the best ways to incorporate PD that moves teachers forward and helps them directly to grow in their practice. Embedded instructional coaching might include an A.M. learning session with an instructional coach sharing a new strategy for a teacher, followed by the coach visiting the teacher and students in the afternoon to provide feedback as the teacher implements the newly learned strategy with students in the classroom.

This might be one of several coaching opportunities during the year or over a short period of time. I've seen both models work. Instructional coaching can have a huge impact when a teacher has several chances over a short period of time (say two weeks or one month) to work directly with a coach to make changes to instruction. First, the teacher needs to be willing to listen to feedback and try some different things within their practice. Second, the instruction should be ongoing to help a teacher continue to practice and develop a certain learning model.

In one of my previous districts, an instructional coach would work with a teacher for two weeks at a time, meeting during prep periods and before and after school to share some new methods and strategies, while also collaborating with the teacher to plan instruction that looked different from what was previously happening in the classroom. The coach would then spend multiple periods in the class co-teaching with the teacher to support students as they experienced the new instructional strategies. As the coach provided feedback, the teacher was able to ask questions and further shift instruction. For teachers who were willing to accept critical feedback and adjust accordingly, I always noticed a significant change in the classroom after the two-week period was over.

Districts who are able to employ instructional coaches can really delve deep into job-embedded PD using such a model. Use those curriculum coaches or tech coaches if they exist in your district and build in opportunities for on-the-job learning.

Learning visits: We often sit in our classrooms without any chance to visit the classrooms of our colleagues. We may see them for a short time at lunch, or for a few minutes during a prep period, or maybe pass in the halls like ships in the night. It might be difficult to incorporate meaningful PD into the few minutes of shared time during the day. One of the most powerful ways around this is a learning visit. There is real capacity for growth in giving colleagues the chance to see what is happening in other classrooms. Consider hosting a monthly learning visit. For twenty minutes before school on these days, you and colleagues set off in teams to visit one another's classrooms. You can have a monthly focus, or keep it open for discussion. If any teachers have mobility issues, you can consider hosting the learning visit online.

Have teachers log in and watch as a colleague shares highlights of their classroom strategies and procedures.

Have teams discuss and take notes about what they are seeing or hearing. If physically visiting classrooms, let each colleague leave a sticky note with something positive that they saw. (Maybe they loved a particular anchor chart or innovative classroom design!) If sharing virtually, have teachers leave positive comments using the chat feature. Provide feedback about what you are seeing in classrooms as well. Teachers will often find wonderful ideas and inspiration simply in seeing what other teachers are doing in their classrooms. Make it a regular part of your PD schedule, and see how it can improve the professional learning culture in your school.

Observations and modeling: This category can be difficult to navigate, but professional development activities that use these strategies often have the most positive impact on instruction and learning. Typically, formal observations are the realm of administrators. They often feel like an obligatory checklist of "the teacher did this" and "the teacher did that," without any meaningful impact on instruction.

Having been on both sides of the table (as both a teacher and an administrator), I can assure you that the formal observations implemented by state mandate have little to do with improving our professional practice. As an administrator, you can try to make lemonade out of the sour lemon that is our evaluation system, but it tends to be a very cumbersome process. So how can we embed observations and modeling to improve professional practice?

Principal Tony Cattani created a culture of professional improvement through peer observation at Lenape High School in New Jersey. He started by asking teachers to think about their superpower as a teacher (while wearing a Superman cape, of course). As teachers reflected on their strengths as a teacher (assessment, growth mindset, lesson design and implementation, and classroom management), they were asked to identify their greatest teaching strength as their superpower. Tony and the staff at Lenape embraced the opportunity for professional learning as part of their school day and began participating in peer observations—twenty-five minutes of observing another teacher, followed by a thirty-two-minute reflection period. During the first four months of implementation, more than 350 peer observations occurred.

The result, as Tony points out:

"One of the most significant impacts is that our teachers are talking about teaching with one another more than ever before and our students are noticing that our teachers are doing what we ask them to do every day—get better!" Again, PD  embedded in what teachers do each day can be a powerful tool for improvement. Read more about the peer observations at Lenape High School by following the link in this QR code.

READI Framework: Alignment

Alignment can be tricky. There are many times when district or school goals don't necessarily align with one another. Teachers within an individual school may be working hard to improve critical thinking skills through math instruction while the school district may be ready to roll out a new language arts initiative with a year-long PD implementation. When this happens, it can be difficult on everyone involved. Teachers know that they need to focus on math instruction while also learning about the new ELA initiative. The school administrator will also recognize that most of the staff's PD time should be dedicated to improved math learning outcomes, while the district's language arts supervisor will want time dedicated to the new initiative.

We all know that with limited time comes limited choice. In this situation, everyone feels a divide. "What should we focus on?" becomes the common refrain among teachers, and two different administrators respond with two different answers. It can be hard as a teacher to go along with a goal that you don't agree with or that you aren't 100 percent behind. The same can be said for an administrator who might be put in the position of presenting professional learning sessions that they don't think will necessarily help their colleagues. From the district viewpoint, it can be nearly impossible to implement something new without teacher buy-in.

PD goals are much the same way, guided by different, sometimes dissenting voices. In districts where the district voice is always the most powerful and always wins out, you may see educators (teachers and administrators alike!) who are frustrated with the direction of district PD. The key is balance, and allowing the district, school, and teacher goals to work in conjunction to ensure that everyone's needs are met.

Starting Point: Is this PD session aligned with district/school goals and educator goals?

If the answer is yes, then congratulations, you have successfully mastered the art of matching teacher goals to those of the school and district. And if the answer is no, then it is back to the drawing board to determine what it might take to align the goals.

Professional development plans: In my school district, each teacher is required to select two to three professional development goals for the year and document how they plan to achieve those goals. Teachers might list a district goal, a school-based goal, and a personal goal, then record a number of different activities that they plan to complete during the school year in order to meet these goals. At the end of the school year, each teacher has to turn in a list of completed hours that "prove" that they met the goals outlined at the beginning of the year.

On paper, it seems like it should work. In real life, teachers turn in their professional development plans (PDPs) at the beginning of the year and rarely look back at them during the year. Regardless of their relation to the three goals, hours are documented by teacher and administrator, and everyone shows that "seat time" has been satisfied for the year. It is a strict exercise in compliance culture. "Here are my goals. Here are my hours. Does it *seem* like I learned this year?"

Instead, we should think about professional development plans (and planning!) differently. Start with a PD planning meeting prior to teachers completing their (state- or agency-mandated) PDPs for the year. Have an authentic discussion about what goals need to be accomplished at the district level and the school level. Then work with colleagues to talk about the types of learning that you would like to take part in during the school year. Work with the ROGUE Leaders in your building to determine who can offer their expertise to the process. Use the ROGUE Leader PD Planning Worksheet (QR code below) to help plan relevant goals.

If you can get away with using this worksheet as your documentation, perfect! If not, use the planning worksheet as a guide for your mandated document, which is probably much longer and more formal. List the goals and activities that you want to take part in. Most importantly, complete the anticipated timeline portion of the sheet, and pick an accountability partner and have them initial your sheet. You are much more likely to follow through on these learning activities once you pick a partner and ask them to hold you accountable. Make meaningful plans that you want to accomplish, not just plans that will be filed and checked off.

Professional development teams: As a classroom teacher, I had the opportunity to represent my school and serve on the district professional development team. One of our main responsibilities was planning a district-wide PD day that took place at the beginning of the year with all district staff (including more than seven hundred staff members from ten different buildings). The chance to plan such an event really helped me as a novice educator to understand what is required to align district goals to purposeful and impactful PD.

The PD team had a teacher representative from each building, as well as district leaders. The administrators often sat back and let the teachers drive the planning and implementation of the day. As a team, we would look at the initiatives the district would focus on for the year, then tie them to the goals each of our individual schools wanted to focus on. Finally, each of the school-based team members shared the wants and needs of their colleagues to ensure that all voices were heard in the planning of professional development. I enjoyed participating on the PD team, and it taught me a great deal about the importance of marrying educator goals to district initiatives.

For more information about starting a professional development team in your school or district, check out this resource from the Four O'Clock Faculty website.

READI Framework: Design

As we've already mentioned, planning for the individual professional learning needs of educators can be challenging at a minimum. This is why consideration *must* be given to educator voice and choice. Only you know exactly what you need to learn. We need to build PD systems that allow teachers to plan and participate in PD, rather than systems that allow PD to be *done to* teachers, as Andy Hargreaves points out in the quote at the beginning of the chapter. One of the easiest ways to provide teacher voice is to build your PD sessions by providing choices. Simply allow teachers to choose the sessions they attend. Reviewing a new technology tool with colleagues? Find a coconspirator and be sure to offer dual sessions at the same time that are open to beginners as well as advanced users. When you offer multiple choices that recognize colleagues' different experiences, teachers feel as if their voices are being respected and honored.

As you look at your PD session, you also need to look at the continuum of choice. This means not just offering any choice, but thinking clearly about the quality and variety of choices that you are able to offer. Many schools use limited choice as their guiding beacon and argue that they recognize educator "voice." While limited choice is better than nothing, consider these three PD sessions on the continuum of choice:

1. All teachers learn about the new restorative practices initiative during a sixty-minute session in the cafeteria with two facilitators.

2. All teachers attend a restorative practices overview for thirty minutes in the cafeteria with two facilitators. Two breakouts will follow, with each facilitator leading a session: Restorative Circles (Advanced) and Classroom Practices in Relationship Building (Beginners).

3. Teachers choose one of three sessions—Classroom Restorative Practices (Beginners), Fostering Positive Classroom Climate and Building Relationships (Intermediate), and Restorative Circles (Advanced)—or have the option of participating in a discussion-based session called Best Practices in Restorative Culture Building at the School Level. The intermediate and advanced sessions will be hosted by facilitators, while the beginner and best-practice sessions will take advantage of staff members sharing their expertise on the topic.

While #2 provides a limited choice for educators by offering breakout options for beginners or advanced learners, some teachers may still find themselves not quite getting what they need. You may find a colleague who is already an expert in restorative circles, or someone who is strong in building relationships but not quite ready for restorative circles. Option #3 takes choice to the next level, providing options for beginner, intermediate, and advanced learners while also introducing a discussion-based session where colleagues can share their expertise. Plan #3 also takes advantage of colleagues who are already experts in the topic.

Incorporating a wide variety of choices, including different options in format, learning style, length, and expertise needed, allows us to honor educator voice. With more tailored programs, teachers can speak up more to ensure their voices are heard. We give everyone the ability to learn at their own pace and comfort level while getting exactly what they need. Simply stated, offering more choices leads to more voices being heard.

Starting Point: Is this PD session designed to provide educator choice and voice?

If the answer is yes, then you have successfully expanded your definition of professional learning, providing many choices and options while giving teachers the ability to have a voice in their own learning. And if the answer is no, then you may need to update your PD plan to incorporate more options to honor your colleagues.

Super Secret Suggestions: In *The Four O'Clock Faculty*, I introduced the idea of using "tip jars" prior to a staff meeting to give teachers choice in what they learn about. The idea is to have teachers leave a marble in opposing tip jars as they enter your learning space for a meeting or PD session. For example, your colleagues might be choosing between presentations on improved questioning techniques or engagement strategies for all learners. The presenter is ready to share both sessions, and once everyone has deposited their marble into one of the jars, you will see what everyone wants to learn about.

Offering teachers a small number of options still provides limited choice, but Super Secret Suggestions takes choice to the next level. As teachers are walking into your next staff meeting or PD gathering, leave one jar (or bowl) on the table entering the room, along with some sticky notes and a pen. The idea here is really straightforward. Anyone entering can write down a suggestion for the topic of the session, fold the sticky note, and drop it into the jar. The teacher who has truly been thinking about questioning techniques can suggest that topic. The teacher who wants to discuss assessment, homework, and equity can bring that to the table. Someone who needs a primer in the latest educational app can recommend it as a topic.

This method, however, truly relies on the expertise within the room. The traditional "leader," whether an administrator, instructional coach, or teacher leader who normally facilitates PD sessions, may not be an expert in one (or more) of the topics chosen. So you will need to count on the experts in the room to share strategies or generate discussion around the topic(s). Even within this strategy, you can expand your options to provide more or less voice and choice.

As the facilitator of the session, you can choose one of the Super Secret Suggestions for discussion and learning or you can choose multiple selections from the suggestion jar and provide more choice to your colleagues. Again, if you choose multiple suggestions from the jar, you might be requiring colleagues to step up and lead discussion or present content strategies based on the recommended topics. While it can be nerve-wracking as a facilitator to enter a session without a set topic, it can be freeing for colleagues to have a voice in what will be discussed. Try Super Secret Suggestions at your next PD gathering!

True learner-centered PD: Much of what is considered professional development in our schools is often driven by district decision-makers who may be out of touch with what teachers truly want and need. A new program is touted to improve test scores in language arts so it is adopted en masse and rolled out to every teacher in the district, even those whose students typically score above the curve on language arts assessments. What teachers may truly need is to reexamine how they can use the ninety-minute language arts block more efficiently and effectively to give students more time to read and write. Again, PD is often *done to* teachers, instead of being centered on their own learning needs and desires.

True learner-centered PD puts the responsibility of learning back on the teacher. Work with colleagues to pick an area of focus for the year. Start with a basic needs assessment. Ask these three questions:

- What is your biggest area of struggle as a teacher?
- What do you want to learn more about?
- What drives you to improve or grow as an educator?

By asking these questions, you might be able to determine an obvious area of focus for the year. My biggest struggle as a young teacher was classroom management. I knew that entering my second year of teaching, I needed to work on classroom management or I wasn't going to survive. As a more experienced teacher, I might have sought to learn more about collaborative math strategies. Once you've identified a focus, you can begin to research and learn more about your topic. Read articles, blog posts, and books about the subject. Listen to podcasts or go see an expert talk about the topic. Delve into your area of focus and try to grow as an educator.

In choosing your area of focus, you are also able to shift your priorities as you learn. You may find that your classroom management struggles have more to do with classroom design than you originally thought. You can pivot to addressing this area and, as you make changes within the classroom, determine if you and students are more successful because of your learning. The beauty of learner-centered PD is that you are in complete control!

READI Framework: Impact

Impact is defined as "having a strong effect on someone or something." We would assume that all of our professional development efforts do in fact have a strong effect on educators, but it is not always the case. Our biggest professional development failures often relate to impact within our classrooms. We are forced to sit through a PD session, and we are quickly shown a dozen technology apps and tools that might be helpful to our students. After forty-five minutes, we shuffle off to another session, where we listen to someone else rattle off fourteen more strategies that we can use to effectively engage our students. A quick lunch break, followed by two more sessions with many more suggestions and resources. You've taken copious notes throughout the day, but by the end of the day, you are on information overload.

Without time to reflect on your learning, practice and explore those new tech apps and resources, or comprehend all of those student-based strategies, you return to the classroom the next day and implement zero of what you learned during the PD sessions. All of it was meaningful and relevant. All of it well-intentioned. But it was designed in such a way that it doesn't allow you to use the learning to actually help your students.

How many of you have ever felt this way before? For those keeping score at home:

That feeling of being overwhelmed and not sure what to do first: 1. Student impact: 0.

As I wrote in *The Four O'Clock Faculty*, "Getting educators to reflect upon and change their practice so that students benefit should be the goal of every PD session." Those who are responsible for planning PD haven't quite figured out how to assess professional development and its impact. We have invented measures like seat time, documented hours, and post-session surveys that ask: What is one thing you learned today? We assume that these factors explain the significance of our PD programs while missing the most important measure out there: student learning outcomes.

We need to begin to think differently about our PD outcomes. Yes, we want teachers to grow as learners, but the ultimate reason we seek this is so that students grow as learners too. Let's determine what needs to happen in order for students to benefit from the professional development that we offer.

Starting Point: Is this PD session ultimately going to improve learning outcomes for teachers and students?

If the answer is yes, then congratulations, you have truly mastered professional development. I award you your black belt in PD. You may move on to other, more glorious pursuits. If the answer is no, then you may need to reconsider how your PD sessions help students back in the classroom.

Smaller is better: A PD session is better if a participant is able to leave with one actionable step they can take back into their classroom the next day. As a presenter or facilitator, remember that smaller is better. Anything you are sharing should focus on a few functional items to help the attendees make a change to their instruction. If you are highlighting technology, delve deeply into one tech tool, and be sure to provide some time for educators to practice using it. If possible, have them use the tool to create something that applies to their current students. If I am able to create something during PD that will help my students, I am then more likely to use that resource in the classroom. For example, during a PD session on parent communication, I shared with teachers how I used Smore newsletters (www.smore.com) to communicate with parents. I also gave teachers about twenty minutes to play around with creating a newsletter. One of my colleagues spent the twenty minutes creating a newsletter template for her students. Shortly after the PD session, she introduced the template to her students, and each week, the students produced a newsletter to send to their parents and guardians, detailing all the things they were learning about! Again, the goal is to provide professional development that actually has an impact on teachers *and* students.

Use the rule of three here to help as you plan your PD session. If you are introducing any more than three items (think one actionable step and two useful resources!) within your session, you might be overwhelming your participants. Just think about it from the attendee's point of view: "I just walked out of a forty-five minute session, and the presenter wants me to complete these three action steps and suddenly become an expert in five new resources." How does that make you feel? It's much better to focus on just a few items that colleagues may see as more manageable. Allow everyone to feel more successful by knowing that they need to do only one thing to start to improve their teaching.

Reflect, reflect, reflect: During any given PD session, you might be hit with multiple ideas, strategies, resources, philosophies, methods, and questions. All of it may be useful and beneficial. The problem we often run into, though, is that teachers don't have time to process the information. You may be so busy listening and trying not to miss a single kernel of information that you overemphasize the details and miss the big-picture implications for your learning. We might see a reflection strategy (also commonly used for students) where the presenter will ask participants at the end of a session: What is one thing you learned today? The attendees may write down their answers on a sticky note or enter them in a digital ticket. This type of exit activity, however, does not allow the educator to truly reflect on what was learned.

I would suggest building in a better reflection model as part of your PD session. Give teachers time to reflect throughout the session. Don't bombard them with information, then squeeze in a reflection question at the end. Try using these prompts during any PD session you might be planning.

- State your most important takeaway from the last ten minutes.
- What impact does this takeaway have on my learning?
- What might I do differently based on this information?
- How might I use this learning to help my students?
- If I had to teach this important information to a colleague, how would I do it?

You can use these prompts or any of your own. Additional prompts can be found on the Four O'Clock Faculty website:

Even more important than the questions is the time that you provide for teachers to actually reflect! In addition to building these questions into your sessions, include more time to think and reflect. Teachers are often given only thirty seconds to think after a reflection question is asked, then bombarded with more information. The simple fix is to set a two-minute reflection timer after each question during your session. This might eat into the time for presenting new material, but remember, sometimes our sessions already border on sensory overload. Slow it down. Build in some two-minute reflection breaks several times during the session and give colleagues the ability to think through what they are learning!

We've covered a lot of information in this chapter. The READI framework can be used to think critically as you plan your next PD session. Remember to always ask, "Is this READI?" as you plan:

1. Is this PD session *relevant* to what educators do each day?
2. Is this PD session *embedded* in what educators do?
3. Is this PD session *aligned* with district and school goals and educator goals?
4. Is this PD session *designed* to provide educator choice and voice?
5. Is this PD session going to *impact* learning outcomes for both teachers *and* students?

Use the review information at the end of the chapter to truly understand and reflect on the five READI questions. You will want to plan PD sessions that are meaningful and will ultimately impact both teachers *and* students. Be sure to use the framework to help you as you plan your next PD day or session. Try incorporating some of the strategies if you are struggling in a particular area, like providing voice and choice to teachers or embedding PD in everyday work. Ask the five questions to determine whether your scheduled professional development will have the significance you are seeking.

Most of all, use the READI framework to reflect on what you want out of your planned PD. Thinking clearly about what PD is will allow it to be more impactful.

ROGUE Leader Reflections

PD Keys

- Think about what makes PD relevant to an educator. Consider that embedding PD into what a teacher does each day is an effective approach to improving instructional craft.
- Align teacher PD goals with those of the district by gathering teacher feedback. Use the feedback to provide teacher choice and voice in the PD process.
- Design PD with classroom impact in mind. PD should always lead to improved student learning outcomes.

A Question to Ponder

Which part of the READI framework do you need to focus more attention on when planning professional development?

PD Checkpoint #2: I Hope You Had the "Time of Your Life!"

When I hear the Green Day song "Good Riddance (Time of Your Life)" on the radio, it often gets stuck in my head for days. As a fifth-grade teacher, I used to make a slideshow of photos for students set to this song so they could relive all the fun and important milestones of their year. Whenever I hear the song now, it reminds me to take time to remember what's important.

You've experienced good and bad professional development. Take a few moments to think about your PD timeline. Get a piece of paper and draw a simple line. Think about the earliest PD sessions you took part in and write them first on your timeline. Add in both good and bad PD sessions you've taken part in. Don't worry about exact dates in your timeline. Finish by jotting down three to five activities at the end of your timeline that include PD that you want to experience. This will help you to think critically about the type of PD you seek moving forward.

What do those types of PD look like?

Create your own opportunities that look similar.

PD Session Planning: Start at the Beginning with an Invitation to Learning

A question that I'm frequently asked is: "How do you get people to engage in professional development?" It's a very straightforward question, but there are myriad answers that help establish meaningful, effective, and engaging PD. The one thing everyone forgets when planning professional learning for colleagues is that the PD starts long before the event even begins. Yes, there are the planning logistics that absolutely must be ironed out before any PD occurs. There are to-do lists that must be carried out in order for your next PD session to be successful. But what I'm referring to here is the feeling that a person has immediately upon learning of your PD session.

It's all about the beginning.

It's that immediate feeling someone has once they learn about a PD session. Is it excitement, nervousness, or a combination of both? Or is it that feeling of angst or anxiety that a person may have based on past PD experiences? Chances are, that initial feeling is going to influence a person when it comes to joining your PD event.

You want to start by convincing people from the moment you notify them that it will be something worth their while.

You may begin by:

- Extending an invitation ("Your presence is requested at our next Problem Solving Summit!")
- Asking a colleague a question that primes them for a learning experience ("Have you had a chance to check out the new app that students are using to share and collaborate?")
- Starting a conversation that establishes the need for a quality PD offering ("I'm glad that you shared that your students are struggling with writing. My students are experiencing the same thing!")
- Having a colleague beg you to share something with them ("Can you please show me how you organize your seating arrangements to improve workflow in the classroom?")

Just know that any successful PD does not begin with the session itself or even the event planning. Extraordinary PD begins when you can convince someone that there is a want *and* a need to learn something new.

So how can you engage colleagues in professional development? Start at the beginning.

Send an intriguing invitation: If you've ever planned an important event like a wedding, a baby shower, or a milestone birthday party, you may know of the time and effort that went into designing the invitation.

In most cases, there is a lot of thought put into what the invitation looks like and how it presents to potential guests. What we should also consider is the feeling that the invitation evokes in the prospective attendee. The same applies to PD. We want to garner the attention and interest of our attendees from the moment they know about an upcoming PD session. Take a few minutes to design your invitation in such a way that it becomes the talk of the lunch room: "OMG. Did you see the invitation Rich sent out for his next PD session?"

Start with design: There are several apps I currently use to create slick graphics and designs for a variety of different projects. I often use these tools to create a save-the-date reminder for colleagues or to advertise our next local CoffeeEDU session. (CoffeeEDU is an informal session where educators get together for a cup of coffee and some conversation. Topics are usually free-flowing, and can range from problem solving to collaboration to sharing resources.) For a complete list of tools, scan the QR code below.

Engage potential attendees when you *create an interactive invitation:* Make your own QR code and embed it in your invitation to ask colleagues to complete a pre-session survey or to share their knowledge on the session topic. Ask teachers to share their biggest success or failure surrounding the topic. Build excitement and passion about the session by tapping into colleagues' personal experiences with the content.

Tap into your vulnerable side: Share your perspective on the topic you plan to deliver to colleagues. I sometimes present a session on engaging students in creativity in the classroom. I usually begin by sharing my experience as a student—one that didn't feature a lot of opportunity to engage in creativity. I try to connect with the content by making it personal. A simple statement or prompt can be intriguing to colleagues: "Join me as I explore why creativity matters. HINT: I never had a teacher who challenged me to be creative . . . and you know how I turned out!"

As you will see below, there are different ways to prime colleagues for what's to come. Create an invitation that combines any of these ideas.

Start with a video message: Think about the most memorable commercials of all time. There are many that probably stand out. Apple has always made memorable commercials, and I can still picture their iPod ad campaign from the early 2000s known as the silhouette ads. You can probably picture the commercials too. Dark silhouetted figures sang and danced against colorful backgrounds while holding their white iPods and earbud headphones. Popular music played as the people moved and showed how exciting it was to use the iPod! Print ads also highlighted the silhouettes using the contrasting white iPod. It was a brilliant way to introduce the new technology, and to this day, the white earbuds can still be seen everywhere as a ubiquitous part of our culture. We can all still remember the commercials and print ads years later. It speaks to the power of a visual to compel us.

Inspire your colleagues by sharing a video message to "advertise" your next PD session! Share the story of why you are offering up a new PD session. Describe what you hope to get out of it and what others can expect from the session. The time and effort you spend describing your PD offering will be well worth it when colleagues are engaged upfront. Nili Bartley, an educator from Massachusetts, shares some great ideas for inspiring colleagues through video on the Four O'Clock Faculty website. Check it out below:

Build momentum through meetings: When I first introduced the idea of a district-wide edcamp to staff several years ago, there were many people who had no idea what an edcamp was. I had to figure out a way to sell colleagues on the idea. My regular face time with the staff occurred every month at our district curriculum meetings in each building. I decided to use five to ten minutes at each meeting to provide an explanation for what an edcamp was all about. The monthly meetings served as a great motivational tool to build toward the district-wide PD event. It helped staff members to understand what the day would be like and gave everyone a chance to ask questions. I also used the time during the monthly meetings to preview some of the sessions teachers would be taking part in on the day of the edcamp.

Starting about three months in advance, the infotainment portion of our curriculum meetings both informed and entertained teachers while also selling them on the power of edcamp. I believe this was one of the reasons that teachers who normally would not have taken to a new method of PD came to love the edcamp concept. Promoting and explaining a PD session or concept months in advance also shows staff that you are committed to it. Everyone knows that you are serious about making it successful. Use other meeting time to sell your PD!

Give everyone a surprise clue: Place a fancy pen in everyone's mailbox with a note attached that says, "Tomorrow, this pen becomes your way to connect with students. Join us at 10 a.m. in the faculty room!" This is a perfect way to kick off a session on writing and blogging as a connection tool for students. Plus, everyone will love receiving a shiny new pen!

Everyone loves a good mystery or a little bit of intrigue. (At least, most people do!) Providing a clue, or series of clues, can be a great way to engage and motivate colleagues to participate in a PD session. Consider drawing people in with a mini scavenger hunt. Teachers can search for several items that they will need for the PD session. The crazier the items, the more teachers will wonder, "What can I possibly need a banana for?" (Simple. A banana serves as the perfect mid-session pick-me-up!)

Using a physical clue or a mental challenge (think impossible question, riddle, or brain teaser) can build interest and intrigue into your session and give some insight into what type of professional development colleagues will be participating in. Again, it also shows that you have taken time to prepare and engage participants before the actual event. Don't forget that the PD starts the moment someone learns about it. There's no better way to build engagement than to create a participatory action upfront, something that the attendee needs to do before they walk in the door. A thinking prompt, pre-session survey, or invitation to engage a colleague before the event allows for participation even before your PD begins.

Combine your efforts: Consider using a combination of all these elements to really bring the wow factor to colleagues. An invitation featuring a QR code linked to a video of you explaining your "why" with an attached pre-session survey question starts engagement with your PD on a number of different levels. You could also send out an invitation that links to a video featuring the first in a series of clues or a scavenger hunt. It could also include a video with information about the session topic. The key here is to bring your passion for the PD to the invitation. Remember, staff members have a million things to do. You want to try to sell them on attending your session or event from the moment they learn about it. Give them a reason to be there! Make it meaningful and worthwhile. But first, *show* them that it will be meaningful and worthwhile.

After all, it's all about the beginning.

Check out a sample PD invitation on the following page that features several of the strategies discussed:

PD Rule #3: Get Involved

There are many educators who sit on the sidelines and complain about the worst of PD. In fact, I was guilty of it myself. I sat by for an entire year and endured irrelevant PD while I complained to colleagues. I did nothing to improve my fate. Was I miserable about it? You betcha. Did I feel powerless in changing the situation? Absolutely. Did I finally stand up and do something to change it? Yup.

The opening quote perfectly sums up our next PD rule: get involved.

Don't be like the educators who sit idly by and let PD be done to them. Work from the inside to make it better. Don't just moan about how terrible PD is in your school or district. Figure out a way to improve it. Start your own ROGUE PD sessions. Share a newsletter of resources that you've learned about. Complaining about professional development won't change your fate, but taking action to make it better will ultimately determine your PD destiny.

At first glance, you may consider your position in the grand scheme of professional development and conclude that you are but one individual who has little influence to change our PD systems. I'm here to tell you, however, that you do hold that power. Being overwhelmed and doing nothing leads to no significant change to the culture of professional development in your setting. Taking action because you are frustrated about the lack of quality PD is the only logical step to help you get past that overwhelming and powerless feeling.

Remember, it takes only one passionate person to begin to redefine professional development.

You can make a difference. You can do something about your situation.

There are no excuses and no complaints strong enough to stop you from improving your professional learning. The only way to make it better is by taking action.

So, abide by rule #3: get involved.

Stay involved. Change your PD paradigm.

Chapter 3

Beyond Buzzword Du Jour and "One-and-Done"

> ## "Keep it simple, stupid."
>
> —KELLY JOHNSON

We've talked about how to begin to shift professional development from its current status as a dirty word. Part of the reason it is still regarded in this way is that PD is often used for compliance. Administrators know that teachers need a certain amount of seat time in order to meet state mandates for professional development. Teachers know that this is how PD is being planned, and so they look forward to "PD days" like a trip to the dentist. It's a vicious cycle in which PD is planned, PD is dreaded, and ultimately, PD fails to deliver.

The failure of many of our current professional development practices is related to the "one-and-done" mentality. A school or district administrator sees the buzzword du jour, knows that's exactly what staff needs to improve, and schedules a speaker on the topic. The speaker shows up, shares the canned presentation, and disappears as quickly as they arrived. The staff listens to an hour or two about the buzzword du jour, and then is expected to take it back to the classroom for successful implementation without any further training or support.

If the session happens on a Friday, it is probably forgotten by Tuesday, swallowed up whole by the actual daily struggles and realities of the classroom.

Well-intentioned? Yes.

A quality presentation? Maybe.

Productive or meaningful? Not really.

Forgotten forty-eight hours later? Absolutely!

If we are to make professional development successful in our educational realm, the goal would be to discover and implement the opposite of the buzzword-du-jour, one-and-done mindset! So what is the exact opposite of this mindset?

While difficult to carry out and realize, it's rather basic. The opposite of a one-and-done is to build and sustain something lasting, like a culture. We need to enable deep learning and meaningful change while building a culture of professional learning within our schools. What does it mean to create an entire culture of professional development within a school or district?

We've already mentioned the importance of delivering quality professional development sessions so that colleagues want to see the good in PD. But building a culture of meaningful professional development based on deep learning can be a pursuit years in the making. If we are to build a culture from the ground up or need to rebuild the professional learning culture in our schools, we as ROGUE Leaders will need to make very careful choices about how we do that. Consider the following advice when trying to build beyond the one-and-done sessions to a school-wide culture of professional development.

Deliberate PD

"Deliberate," when used as a verb, means to engage in long and careful consideration or to consider a question carefully. With many PD offerings, we don't deliberate while planning. We don't often give careful consideration to how long it might take someone to learn about a specific topic. We've all seen sessions where educators are asked to quickly consider something and implement it in their classroom after only forty-five minutes or an hour of professional development. This is not nearly enough time to ensure that we are carefully vetting something before using it with students in the classroom.

What if we extend the time to consider an idea? What if we as educators were more deliberate about how we examine an idea? Or a topic? Or a program? Or a tool or resource?

Consider using multiple professional development sessions for a four-pronged approach to deliberate PD.

1. Address preconceived notions of the topic or idea. This can be done with the whole group first or in small groups before sharing with the larger group.
2. Consider the logistics of the concept or idea. This is the meat and potatoes of what you are talking about. How is it intended to work? What will I need to do as the classroom teacher?
3. Critical thinking about the concept or idea. This is the opportunity to thoroughly vet what you are learning about. It's the chance to ask the questions that challenge the idea or raise a point that no one has yet considered.
4. And beyond: Now that we've begun implementation, what has worked and what hasn't? What are the questions that need to be answered? What challenges do we need to work through together?

The key is to extend the conversation and learning as long as necessary to make the implementation work. It might take several months.

You may need to revisit many times before your colleagues are ready to embrace something new. It's the opposite of one-and-done, but it actually considers how teachers learn, and gives them the time for deep learning.

Learning and Innovation Need to Come from Teachers!

Another way to move away from the one-and-done mentality is to rely on the experts within your ranks. When you count on the colleagues you work with every day, you know that they will be there to provide support and further learning about a topic. Building up teachers to share their own expertise with colleagues also helps demonstrate the importance of professional development to your school culture. You can also extend the professional learning opportunities beyond just your building to rely on experts within the district. In fact, what's better than changing the professional development culture in one building? Changing it in multiple buildings!

I work at a two-section school. Each grade level has two classes. This means that there are twelve teachers, from kindergarten through fifth grade. Collaboration and collegial learning can be difficult when you are staring back at the same person all year long. I recognized this early on and tried to mix up our PD sessions. But again, there are only twelve classroom teachers at any given point. I brought the struggle to one of my colleagues, a principal from another building who was trying to navigate the same issue.

In spitballing ideas, we thought about doing a shared professional development opportunity for the staff members in both of our buildings. In New Jersey, our teachers are blessed to have two days off in early November to attend the New Jersey Education Association Convention. All school districts in the state close on the Thursday and Friday of the first full week of November. The two days off give all teachers the opportunity to attend a large-scale conference with thousands of other New Jersey educators. There are professional development sessions, nationally renowned speakers, technology demonstrations, and an exhibition floor.

This time frame also coincides with Election Day on the Tuesday of the same week. Many schools are utilized as voting locations on this day, and therefore schools also close. In some districts, students only attend school on Monday and Wednesday of that week in November. In my district, school is closed for students all week. Staff attend school on Monday and Tuesday in order to attend professional development sessions. One day is dedicated to a district-wide professional development day, when teachers from all twenty-four buildings gather in multiple locations to learn together. It can be a bit overwhelming, but it helps to advance district initiatives, especially in such a large district.

The second day is dedicated to building-based professional development and is planned solely by the building principal. So, naturally, my colleague and I saw this building-based day as the perfect opportunity to combine our forces and bring both faculties together for a day of learning. The first Edcamp Yardville was a go! (Both of our schools are in the Yardville area of New Jersey.)

As with any change to professional development culture, it had some pros and cons.

First and foremost, it was *different*. It wasn't something that teachers were used to. (This was a pro!)

Second, it was different. *It wasn't something that teachers were used to.* (Also a con!)

We started by gathering everyone in the auditorium of our building for a kickoff message and coffee. The energy in the room was palpable as the teachers who normally did not see each other came together to talk, commiserate, and share ideas. Several different sessions were offered throughout the day, and teachers found some of the sessions to be helpful. The majority of the feedback that we gathered after the event, however, focused on the time that teachers were able to spend talking with grade-level partners from other buildings. Always ready to listen to feedback, we planned specific grade-level meeting times for our next shared professional development opportunity.

Based on the success of our trial, we reached out to a third principal (whose school was in close proximity) and convinced him to join the project. He had already been enlisting our district technology facilitators to work with his staff. We would use our second monthly staff meeting time each month during the school year to gather teachers from the three buildings for a shared PD experience. In order to positively promote the idea, we wanted to choose a name that focused on the idea of teachers learning from each other. PD LIFT was born! (Learning and Innovation From Teachers.) The goal was and is to lift up teachers through shared PD experiences.

The Logistics of PD LIFT

Each month, we rotate schools as the site for our after-school PD.

Sessions are offered as choices. Teachers can attend whichever session they want, or can choose to meet with colleagues for discussions and planning.

Sessions have been facilitated by teachers, district supervisors, outside experts, and our district technology facilitators. The facilitators are responsible for bridging technology strategies and usage with curriculum and instruction.

First we tried offering two twenty-minute sessions, but feedback from staff proved that this was too short a time frame. We settled on one forty-five-minute session where staff members could learn from each other about a new strategy or resource.

The tech facilitators have really served as the backbone of the sessions, helping their colleagues to learn at their own pace. In some months, the three facilitators will tackle one tech tool and address different needs by offering sessions at three different skill levels. In some months, they will tackle three different tech resources, offering options based on interest. In other months, they will provide open, Q&A-based

sessions for different grade levels so that teachers can get the specific help they are looking for.

After gathering additional feedback, we provided time for grade-level and department teams to use the time together on several occasions to plan instructional units. This time became valuable to the teams who normally had only one other colleague to plan with. (During a year when two new kindergarten teachers were hired at the same time in our building, it was a great opportunity for them to share with more experienced colleagues from other schools in the district.)

The End Result

Tweaks and improvements continue to be made to the PD LIFT project. Early on during the process, we used a couple of outside presenters to share some expertise. We quickly realized that while this was initially helpful, it went against our goal of trying to have teachers learn from colleagues they could later reach out to for help with implementation. It's great to think and talk about an idea with a collaborator, bring the idea to the classroom, and then share questions or feedback at the following month's meeting. While PD LIFT is still a work in progress, it has given teachers the opportunity to learn from colleagues they wouldn't normally have a chance to learn from. It has shown that quality PD and sharing needs to be at the forefront of continuous growth and improvement for teachers. It has helped to improve the culture surrounding professional development in all three buildings, and allowed teachers to grow along with colleagues at their own pace.

Is it worth it? Do one and done motivational speakers work?

I've worked as a consultant. I've been the one-and-done speaker brought in to kick off a school year for staff. My presentation is usually two parts inspirational and seven parts practical. I try to share as much as possible for teachers to take back to the classroom with them. Part of the reason is that I've never understood the motivational speaker brought in to inspire teachers. If you need to be inspired to teach students every day, then maybe you went into the wrong profession.

Many high-level administrators charged with these types of things assume that bringing in the big "one-and-done" professional speakers has a huge impact! When I first became a teacher, my district sometimes kicked off each year with a big speaker, someone who was being paid big money to come in and inspire the staff. It was the only time all year that we would see the person. We would sit in the high school auditorium and listen to the person speak for thirty minutes to an hour. Don't get me wrong, there were several speakers who were highly motivating and entertaining.

One time, it was a magician/juggler, who was very funny. The majority of the crowd laughed at the right times and left inspired to start the year. I was motivated and inspired to start the school year, but guess what—even before walking into the room, I was motivated and inspired to start the year. I *guess* I was more excited after leaving?

Would I ever see the ma-juggler again? Nope.

Was it worth the money the district spent? Maybe. Maybe not.

Did it make anyone walking out the door a better teacher? Probably not.

This is the most important part that often gets forgotten when we try to create a huge impact with a one-and-done speaker. The huge impact should be happening in the classroom, not on the district budget sheet or on the faux motivation-o-meter. Inspiration is short-lived. Quality professional learning is not.

Another district I know of brought in a former pro football player. The message was very inspirational. After about forty five-minutes, the speaker finished sharing his message of how important the job of teaching is. The crowd roared to its feet and gave the speaker a standing ovation.

Again, motivational? Check.

Inspiring? Check.

Was it worth the money the district spent? Maybe.

But the more important question is: Did any of those in attendance walk out the doors of the auditorium that day as better teachers? Probably not.

Now I may be putting myself out of a few consulting gigs, and that is OK. The key is helping to push professional development that will have impact on teachers *and* students. We need professional learning to help teachers grow. Quality PD makes everyone in the room better by helping them become better teachers.

Professional Development Doesn't Need to Be Complex!

We get caught up in the complexities of delivering quality professional development. We assume that there have to be a thousand moving parts, and that teachers need to have a personalized, detailed agenda in order for the PD to be meaningful and effective.

Recently, I attended a full-day workshop discussing improving attendance for students. It was a great day, featuring some meaningful discussions about how to improve attendance. During one portion of the day, we were asked to collaborate in small groups to read and discuss some solutions related to the impact on all stakeholders that chronic absenteeism can have. The facilitator gave each of us a copy of an article, and then proceeded to spend five to ten minutes introducing a complicated system of how we were supposed to divvy up the reading and share with each other. Even after the ten-minute explanation, my group still didn't understand the overly complicated rules for reading and sharing. We spent another ten minutes trying to figure it out before we were each able to read a section and share our findings. It was an exercise in complicating things for the sake of complication.

But professional development doesn't have to be complex in order to be effective. It has to be meaningful, and sometimes, the most meaningful activities to engage in are the ones that are the simplest.

Kelly Johnson originated the KISS principle (Keep It Simple, Stupid) while working with the navy in the 1960s. The idea is that systems work best when they are kept simple and not overly complicated. The same thinking and mentality can apply to designing meaningful PD experiences. Remember to avoid unnecessary complexity and focus on simplicity.

Start with these basic structures to keep it simple.

Slow PD: We usually rush from one PD topic to the next, never giving ourselves enough time for deep learning. Slow it down! Gather colleagues together for a discussion-based session, and start with one simple question. Let the participants share for thirty to sixty minutes of deep discussion and meaningful conversation around the topic. The key is choosing a great question to engage everyone. Try one of these:

- Is our assessment and grading system fair to *all* students?
- Are we meeting the needs of *all* students—those struggling, those excelling, and those somewhere in the middle?

What about the children on the fringes who have their own unique needs?

- How can we incorporate more critical thinking skills across all subject areas?
- How can we empower students to take charge of their own learning process?
- What systems or practices within our school(s) are antiquated and need to be fixed? How do we fix them?

An effective PD session can be based on a single question. Remember the KISS principle. Don't overcomplicate things. Sometimes, giving teachers the chance to slow down and deeply consider a single question can be a meaningful way to spend an hour. In fact, maybe what teachers really need is more . . .

Time to talk: A novel idea. Think carefully about how this might be set up. Teachers need time to talk. To converse. To debate. To discuss. To share. To collaborate. Can you help colleagues find time to talk? If so, it could be an answer to several of the problems found in the PD system already in place.

Maybe it's a weekly coffee-and-chat session organized before school with no set agenda or topics. Educators come in, grab their cup of joe, and begin to share with their colleagues. The discussion may run the gamut from complaints and struggles to successes and breakthroughs. Teachers might pose questions about how a particular strategy is working. The key is in the free-flowing nature of the session. Giving teachers time to talk can lead to discovery and improvement.

If it's not a planned time, consider building in other opportunities for conversation and collaboration. In our school, any time we have an extra substitute (or two) around, we provide teachers with the chance to meet for extra planning time. It's often helpful just to give colleagues twenty extra minutes to talk to each other. This time often creates dialogue that can lead to an instructional breakthrough or awesome collaborative project.

In fact, any daily conversation can be an important stepping stone to a breakthrough. Sometimes, when you talk through a problem with a colleague, you figure out exactly what it is that you are struggling with. So find those times to converse. In the cafeteria doing lunch duty? Find time to talk to your colleagues as well as the students. Standing in line for the copier? Talk about what you are working on with students. Walking to the parking lot in the afternoon? Share what your day will look like tomorrow.

Professional conversations and dialogue make us better educators. It's just a matter of finding minutes within our day to have those conversations. The time is there! Let's find it.

Book clubs and #StaffBookTasting: If you are able to schedule a more structured activity to generate professional conversation among colleagues, a book club may be the way to go. Many educators are avid readers, and a professional book can generate meaningful discussion about our practice. In the past, I've participated in and led book studies in a number of different schools with a variety of different books. The best discussions usually happen when the book study remains very casual and informal. Try to minimize mandated required readings of:

- specific chapters or page numbers,
- weekly question prompts, or
- written responses and reflections that must be completed.

Reading is meant to be joyful, not an act of compliance. A professional book club needs to recognize this. I prefer the use of the term "book club" versus "book study" because of this. It establishes a certain informality, and presents the PD opportunity as an enjoyable experience rather than an exercise in obedience and conformity.

Selecting a single book as a point of discussion can meaningfully impact instructional practice among a group of educators. I've seen administrators choose the specific book a club will focus on. I facilitated a book club based on educator suggestions, called Choice Book Club, in my first role as a building principal. I began by offering a survey about which books the staff would like to read. The mistake I made was in selecting all the book choices for the survey myself. We chose one book based on the option that received the most votes in our survey. The discussion that popped up around the book was effective and meaningful, but it could have been more effective and meaningful with a few tweaks.

Based on the success of the book club, I wanted to offer more options of books for colleagues to read. One day I had a conversation with a third-grade teacher who was creating a "book tasting" event for her classroom. (Thank you, Ms. Tirro!) Students would mill about the classroom and explore different book choices in different genres, complete with paper place settings, fancy tablecloths, and snacks. The only thing missing was wine and cheese! I loved the idea and wondered if we could marry the idea to the staff book club idea, and our first #StaffBookTasting was born. Using one of our monthly staff meeting time slots, I set up a book tasting featuring several books that staff had expressed interest in. Each teacher would get to choose a book for our upcoming Choice Book Club.

While I tend toward the simple in my setup of these types of events, I've seen others who took the idea and ran with it, creating elaborate staff book tasting events. I featured simple white tablecloths (of the plastic variety) and plates of chocolates on each table. The event was a hit, and led to an awesome book club featuring positive conversation about several different topics based on the books teachers chose (the pros and cons of homework, student engagement, mindfulness practices, and examining our assessment methods). It was a great way to engage staff in professional dialogue and collaborative learning. Simple, fun, and meaningful at the same time!

For more details and pictures from the first #StaffBookTasting event, check out the post from the Four O'Clock Faculty website.

The Greatest Book Club
There Ever Was!

About four months after it was released, approximately one hundred educators came together using the Voxer app for a book study of *The Four O'Clock Faculty*. The book club was organized by New Jersey educator Matt Larson and was intended to last approximately four weeks.

I was excited to be able to participate with so many wonderful educators and share critical discussion about one of my favorite topics: professional development. Voxer turned out to be the right tool! (Voxer is a phone app that allows you to record and share asynchronous audio messages. Users can listen and share at their own pace, and listen to other messages whenever it is convenient.) From the get-go, participants were able to connect and share their experiences, and the audio messages allowed for conversation to continue throughout the day.

As the group approached the potential end of the book study at the four-week mark, many realized that the discussion needed to continue because everyone participating was experiencing tremendous growth as educators.

"Should we continue this group beyond the book study to talk about other education topics?"

The question was asked and answered quickly. The majority of the group wanted to move forward. The next question revolved around whether we should change the name of the group.

I'm honored that the group decided to move forward as the #4OCFPLN.

Discussion continued well beyond those four weeks. The discussions became more intense and more personal. The discussions started early in the morning (for those on the East Coast) and ended early in the morning (for those on the West Coast)! The #4OCFPLN became a #PLF—a Professional Learning Family!

There was no topic in education that was off-limits. The status quo was challenged. Opinions were challenged. Even though difficult questions were asked, the group remained collaborative, supportive, and positive! In fact, these qualities have allowed the group to continue sharing and learning together three and a half years later, at the time of writing this. The discussion is still vital and continues to push everyone in the group.

I currently have more than 17,000 unread and unheard messages. The group is prolific. They can't stop being passionate about education.

Of course, participants have come and gone, although there are many who have joined because of the impassioned spirit that everyone in the group shares. As a participant in the group, I quickly began to fall behind in discussions. I don't participate on a regular basis anymore but check in when I am able. There have been several mini get-togethers, and I was fortunate to join a number of the #4OCFPLN members for dinner last year.

The simple book club grew from a four-week activity to something way more meaningful. The group of passionate educators known as the #4OCFPLN continues to challenge each other every day. In *The Four O'Clock Faculty*, I introduced the idea of the Relevant Organized Group of Underground Educators (ROGUE). I suggested finding one's ROGUE friends—those who would stretch your thinking and challenge you to become a better educator. The #4OCFPLN is the ultimate definition of going ROGUE.

In fact, almost two years after joining forces, seventeen members of the group traveled from around the country to the ISTE Conference in Philadelphia to share their story about how they took charge of their own professional learning. When I first started writing the original #4OCF book, one of my goals was for educators to do exactly this—take the ideals and spirit of the #4OCF and change professional learning for themselves and others. It was a dream come true that a group of educators would actually live the ideals of the book, and I'm glad they did. That's how they became the greatest book club that ever was.

Professional development doesn't have to be a convoluted and meandering labyrinth in order to be meaningful. Sometimes, it can just be simple. If you avoid one-and-done sessions that deliver little on meaningful results, you can create a culture of professional development that ultimately impacts teachers and students. Don't forget to keep it simple, stupid. Make it better by making it easier to learn. Then keep that learning going!

ROGUE Leader Reflections

PD Keys

- One-and-done PD sessions do *not* help create a positive culture surrounding professional development. Quality PD needs to include chances for deep learning and study.
- Make PD deliberate. Provide opportunities for colleagues to thoroughly examine an approach, while giving them the chance to try it out in the classroom.
- Learning and innovation need to come from teachers. LIFT up your colleagues by collaborating, sharing, and providing feedback.

A Question to Ponder

How can you make your PD process simpler while also improving your capacity for learning?

PD Checkpoint #3: Are You Telling Me You've Built a Time Machine?

When Marty asks Doc Brown this question in *Back to the Future*, he doesn't understand the adventure they are about to embark on. They successfully go back to the future by realizing that you need to be forward-thinking. An interest in what the future holds might inform our present.

Think about all the PD sessions you've been a part of during your career (whether for a short amount of time or for many years). Grab a pen. Now, fire up your DeLorean to 88 miles per hour! Jot down your thoughts to these questions:

What should PD look like in five years?

_____

_____

_____

_____

Ten years?

_____

_____

_____

_____

Fifteen years?

_____

_____

_____

_____

_____

Why wait? Look at the ideas you came up with and figure out how you can make them a reality in the present. Even if you need a little help from Doc and Marty!

PD Rule #4: Bring Your Passion!

As an instructional coach, I was once presenting an after-school workshop on math engagement strategies to a dozen or so teachers. It was part of a new curriculum implementation that our school district had undertaken. I was excited to share several great resources and methods for pushing kids to think critically in math. This topic was a passion of mine, and I couldn't wait to share my enthusiasm with others.

I went to the main office shortly before dismissal and met with the principal to give him an overview of the workshop. I was enthusiastic and let him know I would do my best to help support teachers even after the session. He agreed that this was a necessary topic for staff, and said that he would make an announcement to teachers, informing them that I would be set up in the cafeteria after dismissal. I returned to the cafeteria to finish setting up my materials, and I heard a loud voice boom over the building's PA system:

"Attention, teachers: that district math workshop that you must attend will begin after dismissal in the cafeteria. Rich Czyz will be telling you what you need to do now during math class. It is mandatory for all third through fifth grade teachers. Don't be late."

I hung my head. I knew I was dead in the water. This was already a tough audience, and the principal had just dampened any energy I was bringing to the table. He demonstrated zero passion for this topic, and I quickly realized why the staff might typically demonstrate a lack of interest. The lack of passion was modeled from the top.

PD can't be viewed as something that needs to be completed or checked off a list. This sort of checklist mentality still permeates professional development everywhere.

"We held a session. Check. Now we are done."

In order to improve the culture surrounding professional development, you need to bring passion.

Passion for the content and topics.

Excitement for the format.

A desire to share, discuss, and converse with colleagues about relevant issues.

Professional development simply works better when those in attendance are passionate about what they are learning. Provide choices. Provide engaging sessions. Make them interactive. Challenge others to think deeply. Make PD exciting. Teachers need to be astonished and overwhelmed in the sense that they can't wait to get back to their students to try out something new.

Rule #4: bring your passion.

Passion can be contagious. Ideas will spread. Others will learn. They will become passionate about their own professional learning.

Now's the time. Make it happen.

Chapter 4

Pushing the Pessimists

"What we've got here is failure to
communicate. Some men you just
can't reach."

—Captain in *Cool Hand Luke*

*T*he *Four O'Clock Faculty* started with the idea that sometimes you
need to find your own professional development because there
won't always be someone there to make sure it happens for you. You
might sit through boring and meaningless faculty meetings. You might
attend the dreaded district PD day, which turns out to be a complete
waste of time (six hours that you will never get back). You might try to
do amazing things with PD, only to have colleagues return a
blank stare or roll their eyes at you. Throughout your
career, you will encounter those who look on *any*
professional development experiences with a pessimistic eye.

You could give out crisp $100 bills to every
participant in an audience, and most will be
excited about the fresh newfound cash! You

will, however, still have one or two people who gripe about the fact that they didn't receive $200 instead.

One of the questions I'm most often asked with regard to PD is: What do we do about the pessimists, negative nellies, and naysayers? Those who, no matter the professional development offered, find a way to complain and point out every fault. How do we inspire the unenthusiastic and reluctant to suddenly participate?

I am asked this question all the time and it is one of the most difficult questions I've been faced with. As expressed in this chapter's opening quote, from the movie *Cool Hand Luke*, it can be very difficult to reach everyone. So, then, how do we reach the unreachable?

I've often heard the advice that we should just avoid and completely ignore the naysayers because we will never be able to convince them to engage. I think this misses the point. We need to recognize that the naysayers may only be a small group, but they still provide an important voice in determining whether our professional development activities and strategies are working.

It may seem counterintuitive, but trying to ensure that even the pessimists have a voice actually gets back to the core mission of *The Four O'Clock Faculty*. We want all educator voices to be heard, even those who may bring criticism or negativity to the PD movement we are trying to move forward. Those dissenting voices may have legitimate concerns ("Priorities are constantly shifting from one buzzword to the next!") or be able to share important information ("I'm feeling overwhelmed with the amount of PD on top of everything else!") about why PD is not working for them and may help to improve the professional learning process in the long run.

We also have to recognize that educators who are not engaging in our PD structures may not always be naysayers. They may be finding it on their own or engaging in other ways. Through the years, I have noticed that there are three groups of educators when it comes to meaningful professional development.

The *willing* are those who show up whenever they need to in order to learn. Before-school book club? Yep. Saturday morning and afternoon at edcamp? You betcha. Sunday morning CoffeeEDU? Might be a little tired but sure. The willing gather at every opportunity in order to continue their learning. The willing are the lifelong learners. They have a need to keep pushing forward, to keep asking how they can make it better, to keep collaborating in order to learn something new. Whether they are in their second year of teaching, or have been in it for the long haul, logging thirty-plus years, they still seek out learning to improve their craft.

The *unwilling*. We've talked a little about the naysayers already, so we don't need to share much more about how their unwillingness to engage in anything new can affect others in their search for meaningful PD. However, I'd like to distinguish this group from . . .

The *unable*, who are much like the willing but with less opportunity. They would love to attend the before-school book club but have childcare issues in the morning. They would love to attend that edcamp on Saturday, but family obligations don't allow for their attendance. Some may not be able to attend for health issues or they may lack access. The unable try to squeeze in PD wherever they can. "I can stay for just fifteen minutes today. What are you able to show me in G Suite?" Don't confuse someone's failure to participate in PD opportunities with a lack of interest, want, or need to participate in meaningful PD.

The Professional Development Championship!

Fighting out of the blue corner, from Jefferson Elementary, third-grade teacher Mr. Henry! And fighting out of the red corner, from Franklin High School, biology teacher Ms. Jones! Fighters, touch gloves, and share your expertise with your colleagues. **May the best PD win!**

Shortly after *The Four O'Clock Faculty* came out, I met Stacy Saia online. She reached out to share some amazing work she had been doing in her school as part of ROGUE PD. There was one particular element she shared that blew me away in its simplicity. As a lifelong wrestling fan, I was super impressed. In order to motivate colleagues with regard to professional development, Stacy awarded the #PalmyraRocksPD Championship Belt to teachers in her district (the Palmyra School District in New Jersey). Yes, it's a championship belt of the red leather strap and gold plates variety, and it rivals anything you might see in the professional wrestling, mixed martial arts (MMA), or boxing worlds. (www.undisputedbelts.com can be used to order your own customized PD championship belt!)

Each month, Stacy builds on the competitive nature of teachers to motivate them to participate in various professional learning challenges or activities, and other staff members nominate their colleagues to hold the Championship Belt for the month! A winner is chosen each month based on the professional growth work they have done or are doing with others. The winning teacher is announced at a school-wide assembly featuring staff and students. The importance of learning and professional growth is modeled for everyone. The competition heats up among colleagues and drives professional learning and growth. This is ROGUE Leadership at its best.

May the best PD win!

The winner and new undisputed PD champion is . . .

Now that we understand the parameters of who we are working with, we can better apply principles of high-quality professional development that will hopefully engage everyone. But remember that everyone needs to engage in their own way. The willing will always be there, ready to take on anything. The unwilling will be a little harder to reach, but it's not impossible. The unable will do their best to learn when they can.

Try to engage the naysayers by considering the following factors:

What do you know about the naysayer?

It all starts with understanding the naysayer and where they are coming from. Can you learn more about the naysayer's experience to understand why they are unwilling to participate, contribute, or share?

Begin by asking some questions:

- Is the naysayer really a naysayer? Or does the naysayer really belong to the unable group? (Sometimes frustration can boil over when you want to participate but can't.)
- How long has the naysayer been in education? Are you fighting against their experience of thirty-plus years of bad professional development or just a few bad experiences that established a poor relationship with PD?
- Along this same line of thinking, what kind of experiences does the naysayer have with PD? Good, bad, or indifferent?

- What is the best PD session they have ever participated in?
- What would the naysayer like to do during professional development activities?
- Does the naysayer only act negatively when it comes to professional development? Or are their negative tendencies toward everything related to being a teacher—lesson plans, district initiatives and directives, field trips, and so on?
- Have you ever had a positive conversation or interaction with the naysayer? Is it a possibility? This last question is key . . .

Finding out some background information about the naysayer will accomplish two things:

1. You will learn why there might be some resistance.
2. You will start to build a relationship with the naysayer.

What type of opportunities work for the naysayer?

I've worked with colleagues who presented a different face in front of a larger group of colleagues than they do in a private conversation. I remember a specific colleague saying to me in a discussion away from the larger group, "You know that they look for me to disagree with everything, right? I don't always disagree, but I have to seem like I do." It was eye-opening for me, an interesting position that I hadn't considered. This person saw themselves as the voice of the teachers *against* the administration, the instigator, the one who was *supposed* to disagree and question anything and everything. It made me rethink how I approached my role in PD with this person. You may need to consider that the naysayer has a certain reputation to protect when facing new PD opportunities in front of a group of colleagues. The naysayer may be someone with seniority, someone who has less to lose by expressing criticism, and therefore feels more comfortable in sharing those concerns. Although others feel the same way, they may be less likely to express their concerns based on their position. So, how do you avoid these confrontations and disagreements in front of everyone?

Try approaching the naysayer in a one-on-one setting. Meet with them before you share an idea or activity with the whole group, and explain your "why." Try to understand how they feel about the idea first, and poke holes in the idea with them. This may give the naysayer more of a voice in PD and how it's planned. In a previous district, some of my strongest working relationships in planning district-wide PD were with two of our union leaders, who I knew would ensure that any PD met our contract criteria. I would often go to them first to pitch my idea so that they would provide contradictory ideas or give the opposing viewpoint. Once they explained the problems with my plan, I could redesign, and re-engage them in the planning process. It was a win-win because then I had their buy-in and support when I was ready to share with a larger group. In this way, the naysayer actually becomes a conduit to the people who might feel frustrated by PD but aren't comfortable expressing it. The naysayer becomes an advocate for others and engages in the process by being a naysayer!

How can you plan for (or with) the pessimist?

One of the key factors that might drive the naysayer(s) in your building is finding the faults in the current systems, programs, or initiatives being implemented. As educators, it seems like we have a natural tendency to complain about everything.

Not enough resources or supplies. A class full of struggling students. Too many state mandates. Not enough time in the day. The list goes on and on. Yet, amid all of the complaints, how often do we seek solutions to our problems? We usually don't.

Complaints + More Complaints = Even More Complaints
Complaints + Brainstorm = Solutions

Again, why not try to focus this critical feedback for improvement purposes? Introduce professional development opportunities that embrace criticism and use the feedback to drive learning forward. Consensus building can play a huge role in professional development, as teachers are able to consider the most negative criticisms and really explore why the criticisms exist. Teachers need not only to consider the harsh criticisms but also to propose solutions that will help the whole group move past the negative feedback. Again, this only further engages the naysayer in the process and in improving learning for all.

Try a *negative brainstorming session*. Let educators complain their way to solutions.

Now, you may be asking yourself: How could this possibly work?

Why would we ever want to encourage educators to complain? It seems like it defeats the purpose. Seems to be counterproductive. Because complaints beget complaints. And that's all we need. More complaints.

But the whole idea of the negative brainstorm is that complaints beget complaints. Once everyone starts complaining, you can discover exactly the problems that need to be solved. Then you can get to the real work of solving those problems.

Obviously, we must first start with complaints, but the key is to not let it get out of hand! Start by breaking your large group into smaller groups. Keep each small group at three to five people.

So, how does the process work? Follow this simple procedure for turning your biggest naysayers into your best problem solvers!

1. Complaints need to be logged (large chart paper and markers are best!) and listed with a follow-up question. Give small groups five to ten minutes to log their complaints and questions. For example:

> → **I don't have enough time to complete work with students.** *How can we improve the schedule?*
> → **I am struggling to help our struggling learners!** *How can we improve our basic skills program?*
> → **We don't have enough time for meaningful PD!** *When can we meet to expand our professional learning*

2. Next, have each small group rotate through the room to review all the complaints. Have each group add a check to any complaint they agree with.

3. After each small group has reviewed all complaints, find two or three problems that are common among each of the lists. Focus on these complaints and corresponding questions.

4. Have teachers then choose one of the three chosen complaints or problems to generate solutions. Make new groups.

5. Each group brainstorms possible solutions to their chosen problem. No idea is a bad idea! Remember that the goal is for teachers to take a possible solution to their complaint back to their classroom to try out.

If structured properly, this method will allow you to engage the unwilling, or at least positively harness the negative energy that the pessimist may bring to the table. By engaging the naysayers, you may also just begin to change attitudes about professional development.

I previously worked in a district where the lack of a solid reading program and resources was the biggest complaint of teachers at the elementary level. Teachers were left to fend for themselves to find teaching resources and instructional materials for students. This resulted in a very haphazard system of reading instruction with a wide variety of questionable materials and strategies being used in different classrooms. From an administrative perspective, not having a cohesive plan was a big problem, and from the teacher perspective, not being provided with resources and materials made educators feel like they had to come up with everything on their own.

This served as the perfect opportunity to use a negative brainstorm. Teachers were already coming to the table with things they didn't like about the reading instructional plan in the district. Rather than fight the vitriol directly, we brought teachers together to share their criticisms and gripes, and more importantly, to discuss how we could work together to address some of the concerns. Teachers mainly wanted some common resources that could be used by all so they wouldn't have to spend a lot of time constantly searching for them. For the administrative team, this would also create a more cohesive program that would look similar in different classrooms.

One of the best ideas to come out of the negative brainstorming sessions was the idea of a group of teachers being the ones to curate the resources and providing them with grade-level colleagues. Given time and support by the administration, teachers were able to come up with common resources and instructional materials that were shared with everyone. While the sessions didn't solve all of the problems associated with reading instruction, they did start us on a path of using the criticism to fuel growth and improvement in instruction and learning in the classroom. Providing an outlet for the negativity, complaints, and grumbling actually led to a usable solution that both teachers and administrators could move forward with.

How Do You Innovate PD and Manage the Teacher Contract?

One of the biggest difficulties with innovating professional development can be working within the teacher contract. What if the contract places limitations on what PD can take place? Or how often it's allowed to happen? I've worked in several settings where the union contract placed certain restrictions on how and when quality PD could take place. For example, teachers under contract could only be required to attend two meetings per month. This covered all meetings—both building-based and district-wide. As the person responsible for planning PD for the district, I had to work closely with each building administrator to ensure that we weren't asking teachers to attend more than the number of required meetings per month.

I learned that the best and most efficient way around the contract was to actually work strictly within it. In one of my previous districts, this question was always going to be asked by union leadership: Is this satisfying the contract? So I learned quickly to work directly with our union leadership to ensure that whatever I was planning met contract requirements. An ounce of prevention . . . I was open and transparent about what I was trying to accomplish and how we could work to collaboratively carry out our district PD goals.

Try these steps to ensure that your PD goals are not hampered by the teacher contract:

Establish a strong working relationship with union leadership: Be open and honest. Explain your "why." Collaboratively tackle roadblocks to make sure everyone's needs are met. When planning district-wide PD that affects all union members, consider their needs and preferences and work within any constraints.

Make "voluntary" your new favorite word: Whenever you are offering different PD sessions that fall outside of standard monthly meeting requirements, be sure to include the term "voluntary" in the session description: *voluntary* problem-solving summit for sixth-grade teams. Let everyone know that meetings are not required or mandatory. If the session is worthwhile and relevant, people will show up anyway.

Create a variety of schedule options: Contracted times often complicate PD schedules. Secondary educators are often done earlier than elementary or primary teachers, which can make organizing a nightmare. Provide multiple meeting times that work for different categories within the contract. Give everyone options to meet their needs that also meet contract language.

Be able to compromise: When you are trying to accomplish big-picture PD goals, you sometimes have to be willing to concede on items that may not be all that important. Consider what you are willing to yield in approaching certain PD opportunities. Is there any part that is negotiable? For example, when I was trying to round up presenters for our first edcamp in my former district, I approached several teacher leaders and asked what might entice their colleagues to present. When teachers said that they didn't have time to plan for a session, they mentioned being paid for their planning time for an edcamp session. While I wasn't able to pay them directly, I was able to secure several substitute teachers to cover them for two class periods to plan their sessions. Compromise and win-win!

Bite-Size Chunks of PD

In *The Four O'Clock Faculty*, I compared shifting PD culture to eating an elephant. It needs to happen bite by bite. We need to realize that we are only going to begin to convert naysayers in bite-size chunks. Those who are unable to attend traditional PD opportunities may also be able to participate in and grow from bite-size chunks of PD that occur during unused moments of the school day or that they can access on their own time. Sometimes, we have to be covert in how we begin to shift culture surrounding professional development.

Sneaking in little morsels of professional development can help motivate colleagues (maybe the naysayers and the unable) and create the ever-important culture of learning that we spoke about in chapter 3.

One of the best ways to do this is to utilize the opportunities where teachers may not even realize that they are learning something:

#CopierPD

On any given day, educators stand in front of either copier in our building while they wait for their copies to be printed. If they are lucky, someone else comes in to use the copier, and conversation ensues. If not, they may stand there silently. Minutes pass, but what if you could somehow utilize this normally wasted time?

Why not captivate and engage a colleague while they are waiting for their copies? Enter #CopierPD. Each month, Amy Storer, an instructional coach from Texas, prepares a one-page infographic that gets posted right above the copier. It might include some teacher self-care information, a tech tip, and some other instructional strategies or project ideas. It's a great way to pass the time, which would otherwise be wasted standing, staring at the copier, and waiting. Even if a teacher glances at the mini-poster in passing, and latches onto a tip or idea, they may be willing to take it back to the classroom and try it out! Find some of Amy's examples here:

> **Simple Tip:** Include a QR code to link to any websites or resources so that colleagues can quickly access them!

#PottyPD

This works much the same way, but in a very different setting. Think captive audience! Create a monthly newsletter and share it in each bathroom in the building. Above the sink is a great place, as colleagues are washing their hands for thirty seconds. You could include new websites that you think might be useful, links to podcasts, or educational blogs. Tara Martin shares an excellent blog post about the idea (see Tara's blog post below) and discusses why this method may be more effective than actually emailing the same newsletter.

Spoiler alert: most educators won't read the emailed version of the newsletter, but they have to as they are stuck in the bathroom.

The other fun part of #PottyPD is coming up with an awesome name for it. I've seen some creative ones like "Learning in the Loo" or "Bathroom Briefs," or you can come up with your own version. Anyone up for a little "Powder Room PD" or "Lavatory Learning"?

> **Simple Tip:** Be sure to share your #PottyPD information in a plastic sheet or case!

A PD Challenge!

November is a particularly crazy month in schools in New Jersey. As mentioned previously, many districts are closed for Election Day and/or Veterans Day, and the New Jersey Education Association Convention closes schools on the first Thursday and Friday of the first full week in November. My school district shuts down for students for the entire week and offers PD opportunities for teachers. Then, a week and a half later, schools close for Thanksgiving break, and before you know it, December rolls in. Many refer to it as "No-School November." It's a lot of stop-and-go, and it can be difficult to gain any momentum.

So, a few years ago, I was struggling with this exact question: How can I motivate staff to take part in meaningful PD when we are barely in school? Does the extra time off provide extra time for PD? And our Never Stop Learning November Challenge was born. Twenty-one different activities that staff members could complete on their own time. Some of the tasks included:

- Listen to a podcast
- Attend a mini PD (ten to fifteen minutes on one tool or topic)
- Read a blog post
- Host a brainstorming session with a colleague
- Write down ten higher-order thinking questions for an upcoming unit
- Visit a colleague's classroom and borrow an idea
- Start a reflection journal
- Learn about a new app or tech tool

After a staff member completed one of the tasks, they could have an "accountability partner" initial a sheet to show that they had finished. As an added bonus to the learning taking place, I offered several incentives to entice more participation. Completing five tasks earned a free dress-down day. Ten tasks earned a chance at a $25 gift card, and fifteen tasks earned a free coverage period. I would schedule a time with them and cover their class for forty minutes while they got in some extra planning or just zoned out for a short while. Teachers got much-needed rest, and I was able to spend more time with students!

Gamifying PD in this manner created a bit of competition and camaraderie among staff, and allowed us to continue learning during the usually lost month. It was a great way to sneak in lots of different types of PD while hopefully motivating colleagues, and even enticing the pessimists to find something that they enjoyed.

Learn more about PD challenges here:

Find a copy of the template to create your own PD challenge here:

> **Simple Tip:** Many local businesses are willing to donate gift cards if they know they will go to a deserving teacher.

PD-mail (It's Not Just Email!)

The first email message was sent in 1971. Here we are fifty years later, and email has changed our lives forever. Some will see it as the bane of our existence, while some recognize the power in its simplicity. (At least those who use it correctly. I'm talking to you, reply-all fanatics!) Other tools and messaging systems have come and gone, and yet, after all this time, we are inundated with emails every day. It is because, at its core, email is a system that works. Take advantage and turn your email into PD-mail!

Once a week, send a quick email with a PD tip, trick, or resource. The key is keeping it simple and short. No one wants to read several paragraphs. We are trying to push the pessimist, not anger them even more. Principal Jay Billy from New Jersey uses PD-mail to conduct a book study! He reads the book for his staff, then emails the most important snippets to teachers each week.

Reading a book without reading a book! What an easy way to conduct a book club with colleagues.

> **Simple Tip:** Be sure to limit your PD-mail to a sentence or two, definitely no more than three! Check out the example below.

From: 4oclockfaculty@gmail.com

To: All Users

Subject: PD-mail! Week #1

Did you know that you can have students create a "podcast" using Google Slides?

Just have students add an audio file to a slide for each "segment."

Learn more here: fouroclockfaculty.com/2020/04/pbl-ideas/

Transforming the pessimistic attitude may be the most difficult part of changing professional learning culture, but again, it's important to engage all voices in the PD discussion. While it might be easier to ignore certain pessimists, we need to have all involved in order to move our profession forward. Get to know the naysayers. Find what moves them. Work with them to discover new ways of growing together. Provide extra opportunities for the unable to participate as well. Sneak bite-size chunks into everyday activities. Shift the culture with a little step by a little step, but be sure that you attempt to bring everyone with you! The ultimate goal is to make PD accessible for everyone—the willing, the unwilling, and the unable!

Try to make PD work for everyone.

Everyone. Including the naysayers! After all, ROGUE Leaders come in all shapes, sizes, and attitudes.

ROGUE Leader Reflections

PD Keys

- You will always find naysayers who take a pessimistic viewpoint of PD. Find ways to use this criticism and negativity to improve PD practices.
- While some educators are unwilling to engage in meaningful PD, keep in mind that some are unable to engage due to their circumstances.
- Use bite-size chunks of PD to build a positive professional development culture. Make PD an overt and ingrained part of daily activities.

A Question to Ponder

What steps or actions can you make to move colleagues in small increments along their own continuum of professional learning?

PD Checkpoint #4: PD! It's Fantastic!

If you are a big NBA fan like me, you count on your starting five to make sure your favorite team wins each night! There is nothing more magical than seeing the team in complete unison, one individual playing the part of maestro and the others playing their individual roles to come together in victory.

Professional development works the same way. You need to be able to count on others to ensure that everyone benefits. Take a moment and identify your PD starting five.

Write down the names of those individuals you will count on to make sure that your PD is meaningful and relevant.

1. _____

2. _____

3. _____

4. _____

5. _____

After you have your list, reach out to them to plan your next PD session!

PD Rule #5: Find Others Willing to Join Your Pursuit

It's not going to be easy. We just learned that there will be those pessimists who are not interested in changing the status quo. If you try to fight the good fight all by yourself, you may quickly realize how difficult shifting the system can be. Can you make a difference all by yourself? Absolutely. Might you burn out in the process? Probably.

Make it easier on yourself by becoming a recruiter. Be a ROGUE Leader. Find those others in your circle of colleagues who are also tired of problematic PD. Convince them that you can tackle the problem together. Build a small army of the willing.

Find a partner and host a voluntary PD session for colleagues. Those who show up are probably the people you want to start with. If you and your partner have only one person show up to your PD gathering, then you've got three willing participants.

It's OK. Start small. The next time you meet, have each person convince one more person to join. As the numbers slowly increase, you will build momentum toward better professional development.

If you can't find your ROGUE friends in your own setting, go elsewhere. There are like-minded individuals ready and willing to collaborate. Start a CoffeeEDU session in your area. See who shows up. Share ideas. Collaborate on projects. Take those meaningful projects back to your students. Continue to share. Spread the word on social media. Use collaborative tech tools or online learning spaces to continue planning and participating in meaningful PD. Distance is not an acceptable excuse for not finding your people.

Rule #5: find others who are willing to join your pursuit.

They are out there, just waiting to be called upon. They are willing to do the work to make PD better. It's your responsibility to find them and lead them.

Chapter 5

Switching Up
Staff Meetings

"A manager's ability to turn meetings into
a thinking environment is probably an
organization's greatest asset."

—NANCY KLINE

Many are suffering. We've all seen the symptoms. Tendency to
check out. Extreme boredom. Lack of participation. Drowsiness.
Not listening. Not showing up. Feeling defeated and sometimes broken. Unfortunately, even after learning that there are better ways, many
of our colleagues and fellow educators may still be struggling with SMS
through no fault of their own.

Staff Meeting Syndrome

Staff meeting syndrome (SMS) is a reluctance to
actively and meaningfully participate in professional learning opportunities due to being
subjected to bad PD. In some cases, people
have had years of exposure, or they may have
undergone a shorter time frame of negative PD
experiences. Regardless of the level of pain or its

duration, many educators have been stricken with some form of SMS at some time in their career.

Even when presented with quality professional learning opportunities, those suffering tend to shy away, keep quiet, roll their eyes, or simply tune out.

While it may seem like there is no help for those suffering, the only assistance we can offer is to continue planning and sharing meaningful PD opportunities with them. Let's continue to expand our definition of what's possible with professional development.

If you come into contact with someone suffering, or if you are afflicted with SMS yourself, it's important to try several steps on the road to recovery. We need to find PD opportunities that allow educators to engage meaningfully, to participate fully, and to go ROGUE if need be. We must realize that PD participants don't need to suffer any longer.

One of the best starting points for shifting the professional development paradigm is staff meetings. Though for too long they have been considered the bastion of bad PD, staff meetings provide a regularly scheduled opportunity to improve learning outcomes in the classroom by helping teachers to grow. And too often, they are *still* utilized for checklists, logistics, and mandated content. All is not lost, though. There are many educators who are using staff meetings to provide meaningful learning opportunities. When you have a consistent chance to help educators grow and take the opportunity to do so, magic can happen.

Try some of these activities to continue switching up your staff meetings in order to bring the magic:

Podcasts and Pedometers

I was recently speaking with a group of undergraduates about how they continue their own professional learning. I was extolling the virtues of podcasts, and sharing some of my favorite series and episodes. I asked the group how many of them listened to podcasts and was shocked when not a single person raised their hand. After reflecting on it, I came to the conclusion that I might be in the minority. Yes, I listen to podcasts every day, and I have several colleagues who listen to podcasts every day, but I also know many people who have never heard a podcast and go on about their day just fine. But podcasts can be an awesome way to learn something new, and they can be listened to during minutes that otherwise wouldn't be utilized to learn (your morning or afternoon commute, washing the dishes, cleaning your bathroom, and so on).

The *Most* Obvious Question: What's a Podcast?

If you are unfamiliar, a podcast is an audio file that can be listened to via your computer or phone. It usually contains episodes in which interviews may take place, or the host may share something about a new topic. There are education podcasts, as well as podcasts on every topic under the sun. Episodes typically are released weekly, biweekly, or sometimes monthly.

In one of my previous school settings, I encouraged staff to continue their learning through the use of podcasts. I would share a recommendation in my weekly Friday update to staff but didn't find that many were actually listening to the episodes. That's when I came across a blog post from Meredith Akers describing Podcasts and Pedometers.

It seemed like the perfect way to allow colleagues to learn more about how beneficial podcast listening could be.

During a Podcasts and Pedometers session, teachers walk and listen to a podcast, hopefully learning something along the way as they get their steps in for the day. When I suggested a session to our staff, I wasn't quite sure what the reaction would be. Several staff members asked the obvious question: What is a podcast? After I felt I had adequately described what a podcast is, I began to think about the logistics for our session. Because I had discovered the blog post in the dregs of New Jersey winter, we waited a little while to get our group up and running (well, walking, anyway). We started our first session on a chilly April morning. I was hoping for some higher temperatures, but a group of seven or eight dedicated souls put on their warmer jackets and joined us to listen to a podcast. Each person chose their own podcast and listened and walked around our back playground area. We walked for about twenty to thirty minutes before the school day began, and we left five minutes at the end of the session to briefly share what podcast each of us had listened to and what we learned from it. Our first session was a success, and we managed to squeeze in several more sessions throughout the spring. Using a staff meeting to introduce the Podcasts and Pedometers concept can be an excellent use of time, getting teachers up and moving and giving them the chance to learn something new.

Possible limitations:

Many staff members have other obligations that require them to participate during a specific time frame. Some can only attend if the session is offered in the morning. But others are only able to take part in the afternoon. Some prefer Mondays, while others want Wednesdays or Thursdays. When this occurs, the solution is offering multiple sessions on varying days throughout the week. Variety is the spice of life. Provide a number of opportunities to join in and create a shared document where each staff member lists the podcast episode they are listening to and a one-sentence takeaway.

Some staff members may have mobility issues that don't allow them to participate. Not everyone will be able to walk while listening to a podcast. Adapt the activity to address this circumstance by allowing participants who aren't able to walk to sit nearby while listening to the podcast. Everyone can then participate during the five-minute sharing session!

Fifteen-Minute Standing Meeting

Is your building administrator reading from a painfully long agenda list of boredom and compliance? Is your district supervisor reviewing testing protocols and new assessment procedures that aren't relevant to you? Is an outside consultant indoctrinating you with information that doesn't even apply to the subject area that you teach?

If you feel like you are wasting time at staff meetings, chances are you are right. A typical staff meeting might last forty-five minutes or one hour, but it probably could be accomplished in less time if the fluff were eliminated. Why does the meeting need to be that long? The simple answer is: *it doesn't.*

The standing meeting is genius in its simplicity. No one wants to stand at a meeting for more than fifteen minutes. The rules are simple. Gather everyone at your next meeting. Set a timer for fifteen minutes. All stand and form a circle. Everyone gets to share an update. It could be something they are working on in their classroom. It could be a question they are struggling with. Perhaps someone has an idea and is looking for partners who want to collaborate on it. Maybe a colleague wants to share and celebrate a success! Every thought, question, idea, pitch, or recognition is greeted with a respectful ear from the rest of the audience, because don't forget, you're still standing.

The key to the success of the standing meeting and respecting the clock is the "pass." If you don't have something to share that is valuable to the rest of your colleagues, you simply pass and move on to the next person. This saves everyone time. Eventually, even the most long-winded of your colleagues will learn to edit in order to keep the meeting short, efficient, and valuable. It can be a great way to ensure that your next staff meeting is productive!

Check out Edutopia for the inspiration for fifteen-minute meetings:

Possible limitations:

My staff is incredibly large, and there is no way that we can all share in just fifteen minutes. If you run into this problem, consider breaking the staff into smaller, more manageable groups. Then have each group report their takeaways via a shared document to the rest of the staff. Mix up the groups each month so that everyone has a chance to meet and discuss with a variety of colleagues.

Some staff members may have mobility issues that don't allow them to participate. If staff members have mobility issues, you may need to adapt the activity. You can simply accommodate those who are not able to stand by providing chairs, or you could introduce a simple, non-standing fifteen-minute meeting. The idea is not necessarily just about standing for fifteen minutes. The key is to learn to edit the meeting down to the bare essentials. Provide an environment where all participants will be comfortable standing or sitting, but focus on the timer and fifteen-minute countdown to keep everything brief!

Mediocre PD

We've all sat through bad PD. But have you ever had to sit through mediocre PD?

There's just enough bad to stop it from being good. And there's some good that keeps it from being completely bad.

It's the kind of professional development that hides behind a mask that appears to be beneficial.

The planner will argue: "But teachers had *choice!*"

You will see through it. Of course they did. It's just that all the sessions still sucked, because they were not meaningful or relevant to teachers' roles.

The planner will double down: "We brought in a world-class outside presenter!"

You know better. Of course you did. It's just that teachers won't ever see that presenter again, and the impact is short-lasting.

The planner will grasp at straws: "We showed a powerful video before we went into our agenda items!"

You've been here before. And now, everyone is better off for having watched the video and listened to the agenda items, right?

Unfortunately, some PD planners believe that including choice or using technology or other measures automatically guarantees good PD. And it doesn't. Including these things sometimes just makes PD mediocre.

Go for engagement. Make sure that whatever is being used, whether choice or technology, conversation starters or chart paper, is deployed in such a way as to engage participants. Give them something to sink their teeth into, and provide something that they want to enjoy learning about.

Go for meaningful and relevant. Give participants not only a reason to want to be there but a need to be there. Build the session so that it has an impact on what the educator does in their classroom each day. Give the teacher a reason to take the idea back to their classroom to influence students.

Go for long-lasting impact. Make sure that what you present isn't intended to be a quick, one-shot boost to a teacher but rather something that will have an impact over time. Avoid the one-and-done. Plan for something meaningful that a teacher might have questions about after they try it in the classroom. Make it an ongoing conversation about how to improve instruction and learning in our classrooms.

No one is looking for the middle of the road. No one is looking for unremarkable and uninspired. No one is looking for something fair and forgettable.

Nobody wants mediocre PD.

Go beyond mediocre.

Chat Stations

Jennifer Gonzalez from The Cult of Pedagogy blog and podcast shared an awesome idea to use with students called "chat stations":

Usually, it takes a great deal of time to create materials and resources for typical stations in the classroom. You may also have to switch out the station objectives several times during the year. Chat stations focus on using strong questions to engage students in discussion within each station. It saves time on creating resources and materials and allows you to change the conversation points for students more frequently.

While the idea works well for students, it can serve as an awesome staff-meeting session to model its use for students. Staff move from station to station with discussion topics. The key is setting up a simple structure to allow for deep discussion. Choosing the right topics is the most important part of a successful session. The session is easy to implement while creating meaningful conversation for staff. It also helps to display a great instructional model for colleagues. I recently used this format during our opening-day staff meetings to kick off some important conversations for teachers surrounding student engagement, family engagement, and goal-setting for the year.

A possible limitation:

Colleagues will not discuss what I want them to talk about. This is inevitable. At any PD opportunity, conversation will veer off-topic. Especially if the topic lacks meaning to the participants. Your job in facilitating chat stations is to ensure that the discussion topics and questions are captivating. The questions need to be so interesting and inviting that teachers will *want* to discuss them. Spend time developing quality questions. Get teacher feedback and buy-in by soliciting question topics. It will be worth the effort! (In fact, this goes for any PD session you are developing. Create engaging, meaningful, and inspiring content to ensure interest in your session!)

Chopped PD

One of my favorite television shows is *Chopped*. For those who are unfamiliar, four chefs are selected to compete and given several baskets of four unknown ingredients. During each round, the chefs have twenty to thirty minutes to take one basket of unknown ingredients and make an appetizer, an entrée, or a dessert. After each round, one chef is "chopped" (eliminated) until the final two chefs compete by making dessert from the final basket. One final chef is "chopped," and the last chef standing is declared the winner and awarded a cash prize.

I love the show because I am always impressed by how the chefs think on their feet and deliver amazing meals to the judges in a short amount of time, drawing on all the skills and knowledge they have acquired during years of cooking, but also by focusing on what they are given to work with.

In trying to continue to make our staff meetings fun, meaningful, and relevant, I introduced our staff to Chopped PD at one of our after-school faculty meetings. The staff was divided into several teams (three to four people for each team) and given a mystery set of "ingredients"—content that teachers would soon be teaching, and a description of analog and technology tools at their disposal to plan the lesson. Each team had to create a lesson from the mystery ingredients. After several minutes of creating, each team shared their lesson idea with the rest of the staff. We voted on each lesson and picked a winner for each grade level. Teachers also had the opportunity to then use those winning lesson ideas as they planned the upcoming content they would be teaching.

For example, when provided with the following basket "ingredients"—

Must-have items: a picture or chapter book

Pantry items: any technology tool or resource

Learning content: acknowledge differences in the points of view of characters, including by speaking in a different voice for each character when reading dialogue aloud

---

—teachers came up with a great lesson idea involving the picture book *The True Story of the Three Little Pigs*, written by Jon Scieszka and illustrated by Lane Smith, and the video recording tool Flipgrid. Teachers were set to engage students with the book to compare and contrast points of view with students. When brainstorming during our Chopped PD session, a group of third-grade teachers came up with a proposal to have students use Flipgrid to record contrasting videos of themselves reading dialogue from the point of view of the Big Bad Wolf from the traditional three little pigs story as well as from the point of view of Alexander T. Wolf from the *True Story* version. Hilarity ensued, and students were engaged by inhabiting contrasting points of view and by speaking differently for each version of the character. The Chopped PD session gave teachers the opportunity to think differently about the lesson and generate an awesome lesson idea that captured students' attention!

While my staff Chopped PD competition was relatively low-key and simple to implement, others have taken the concept much further. Mandy Ellis (@mandyeellis on Twitter) detailed her ChoppED Staff Meeting, which included actual cooking tools, chefs' hats and aprons, and mystery  tools in creating their lessons. All of these tools were used to inspire teachers to create a lesson that they could later use with students.

Whether you are looking for a simple idea for switching up a staff meeting at the last minute or creating a bigger experience for teachers, Chopped PD can serve as the perfect hook to capture colleagues' attention and to introduce some new tools and ideas into your teaching and learning environment.

A possible limitation:

Some colleagues may not like the spontaneous or creative nature of Chopped PD. Those who profess their non-creativity may not feel comfortable engaging in this type of activity. They may not like taking creative risks in front of a group of colleagues. Consider sharing the "mystery ingredients" ahead of time with certain staff members who might be reluctant.

Walk, Talk, and Reflect

Some of history's greatest thinkers and creative geniuses have one thing in common: they enjoyed the daily ritual of going for long walks. The time in nature allows a person to get away from the grind, to think clearly, and to keep active. Several educators have taken this powerful notion and applied it to their staff meetings. Former principal Mark French from Minnesota used walking staff meetings, presenting several topics that colleagues can walk and talk about. Midway through the meeting, partners shift to gain different perspectives from other colleagues. Former principal James Moffett invited staff to participate in a weekly reflection walkabout, where after school on Fridays, a teacher would join a colleague (one they didn't get to talk to all that much during the week) and walk with them for five to ten minutes to reflect upon their week. Try setting up reflection walkabouts in your school. Match colleagues up with partners, and provide these three simple questions as a starting point:

1. What went well this week?
2. What did not go well this week?
3. What will I do differently next week?

Ending the week with this type of reflection activity can provide colleagues with a much-needed boost of reflection headed into the next week!

Possible limitations:

Educators may want to head right home on a Friday afternoon instead of staying for an additional reflection period. This is understandable. After working an incredibly long week, it might be difficult to encourage colleagues to want to stay behind on Friday afternoons. Offer some alternative options. Give those educators who want or need to head right home on Fridays a journal to reflect in. They can reflect for five to ten minutes once they arrive home, and journal their reflections. Offer up a time on Friday mornings to reflect upon the week, or invite staff members to join a reflection session on Monday mornings before the week begins. There is nothing better than a brisk Monday morning walk to kick off your week the right way!

Some staff members may have mobility issues that don't allow them to participate. You may need to adapt the activity if staff members have mobility issues. The key here is being able to share, reflect, and enjoy or be inspired by nature. If some colleagues are not able to take part in walking, provide a simple choice of walking and sharing or sitting outside in nature to reflect and share. Provide an environment where all participants will be comfortable, walking or sitting but still enjoying the inspiration of being outside instead of stuck in the stuffy auditorium or cafeteria for your meeting session.

No shoes. No shirt. No staff meetings?! No problem.

I was leading a Twitter chat on shifting professional development practices. It started with a message from Chris Dodge, an elementary school principal from Massachusetts, suggesting that he was planning on getting rid of staff meetings for the following school year. When I first read the tweet, I was taken aback. Of course you need to have a monthly staff meeting. How else can you help colleagues to grow professionally unless you gather them together to share, collaborate, and learn together? The district has specific compliance rules about making sure that everyone add their name to the sign-in sheet each month.

Then I read the second, more important part of the tweet. "I am planning on getting rid of staff meetings next year. All teachers will have an hour a month to learn on their own. Going rogue!"

Now it made complete sense. Teachers do need more time to learn on their own, and what better way to make it relevant and meaningful than to give teachers an hour back and have them figure out their learning on their own? "Going rogue" is absolutely right! A true demonstration of the Four O'Clock Faculty principle of letting teachers take charge of their own professional development. I needed to know more, so I reached out to Chris and asked him to write a guest blog post for the 4OCF website.

Chris established his premise with the first sentence:

> This is not a blog about getting rid of staff meetings. This is about rethinking staff meetings, PD, and whether we as leaders are practicing what we preach.

The rest of the post outlined Chris's motivation:

> We are very good in schools about pushing for change but the problem is that we are usually adding to the pile of the already lengthy list of obligations and initiatives, and then we wonder why teachers feel that they can't possibly take on one more thing to learn . . . We also must allow them the time and space to learn, experiment, fail, reflect, learn, and grow. If we are truly serious about preparing our students for a personalized world, it is our job as leaders to personalize the learning for our staff. It is time that we offer staff the same opportunities that we want them to offer our students: choice, autonomy, room to fail, reflect, and time to learn with and from their colleagues. This cannot and will not happen by decree or expectation by the leader; it happens when we make dedicated time to do the work.
>
> Taking things off the plate of teachers sometimes just means we have to take a critical look at long-standing practices and consider their purpose and their impact. For me, this meant staff meetings and professional development. I didn't come to this conclusion quickly but one day it dawned on me that I was working really hard with teachers to redefine learning in the 21st century but here I am, holding a traditional staff meeting each month: sitting as a large group and moving through our planned agenda.

It dawned on me while first reading Chris's draft that while I was trying to shift the priorities at staff meetings, maybe it was possible to redefine them completely. Yes, staff meetings could go the way of landlines and the Walkman—once useful but no longer relevant! You, too, can get rid of staff meetings, as long as you replace them with something meaningful and relevant for your colleagues. If you are an administrator in charge of monthly staff meetings, you can cancel them to give teachers the precious gift of time. Be a true ROGUE Leader! Let them determine what they need. Let them find their own learning. Give them resources and support, and let them fly!

Check out the complete post from Chris Dodge:

Now What?

You've read some of these ideas and you are inspired. You want to try one out immediately, or are already thinking of ways to put your own spin on one of the activities. Now that you know some different ways to switch up staff meetings, the hardest part might be the implementation.

If you are a school administrator and responsible for planning staff meetings, you have no excuse. No longer should you be standing in front of everyone seated at cafeteria tables, delivering painful monotone agenda-driven drivel. It's time to switch it up! Pick one of these strategies and bring it to colleagues at your next meeting. Try something new. Learn from it. Make mistakes, and let everyone learn from them. Share. Discuss. Collaborate. Do something different.

No agendas. Just learning.

If you are not an administrator, you may have a more difficult time approaching this type of PD shift. Start by sharing this book (and *The Four O'Clock Faculty*!) with your administrator. Give them options. The not-so-secret secret that every administrator wants you to know:  building leaders cannot be responsible for PD alone! We want and need help. Offer an activity from this chapter, or create your own way to switch it up. (One-page step-by-step directions for each activity and other resources can be found on the Four O'Clock Faculty website. See QR code.)

Share your idea for the meeting and give them a copy of the one-pager. If your administrator is unwilling, host your own ROGUE meeting. Don't let staff meetings drag you down any more. Go ROGUE and go learn!

ROGUE Leader Reflections

PD Keys

- Colleagues may suffer from SMS (Staff Meeting Syndrome) after years of exposure to negative PD experiences. Provide them with opportunities for meaningful, relevant learning instead.
- Staff meetings are not meant to be a laundry list of agenda items. Don't let another meeting opportunity go by without including purposeful professional development.
- Look at staff meetings carefully to figure out if they are the best use of teachers' time. If not, change the structure (or get rid of them!) to better utilize the gathering occasion.

A Question to Ponder

What suggestions or strategies would you use to turn your staff meetings into powerful professional development opportunities?

PD Checkpoint #5: Take a Step Back in Order to Go Forward!

I remember playing the video game *Frogger* as a kid. The goal was to help a frog cross an extremely busy road. You would always plan out your path to have your frog cross the road to safety. Suddenly a truck would lay waste to your best-laid plans. And it was always the timing that did you in. You had to perfect your timing! Sometimes you had to go back in order to go forward.

So, how do you perfect your timing when it comes to PD? Consider the amount of time a diverse group of educators will need to learn about your topic.

Think about your next planned PD topic. Write it here:

_____

_____

_____

_____

_____

Go back to go forward. What type of experience (or lack of experience) is your audience bringing with them?

_____

_____

_____

_____

_____

_____

How much time will a novice need to learn about your topic?

_____

_____

_____

_____

_____

_____

How much time will an expert need to expand their knowledge of your topic?

_____

_____

_____

_____

_____

_____

What types of activities will you use to differentiate between the levels of experience?

_____

_____

_____

_____

_____

PD Session Planning: What to Do with the Middle? Change the Dynamic and Change Mindsets

You've probably never heard anyone exclaim their excitement for the middle. When they are excited about a new movie, moviegoers may talk about the thrilling opening or the surprise ending of the movie. Rarely will you hear someone proclaim, "That was the best middle of a movie I've ever seen." Maybe you are a middle child and lament your experience because your older and younger siblings always garnered more time, effort, and attention. The middle of the week can also be a struggle, as it doesn't have the same fanfare as Monday or Friday. In fact, we try to survive Wednesday by dubbing it "hump day," another day closer to Friday and the end of the week.

There simply isn't a lot of excitement about the middle. But I hope to change your mind.

We've talked about the importance of establishing your PD session or event from the beginning. Yes, it's important to kick off with a bang to gain interest and engagement. But once you have everyone engaged, you need to follow through in order to make it meaningful for attendees. Hopefully, you realize that the real work is done in the middle.

In fact, it's all about the middle.

The middle gives you the opportunity to deliver the meat and potatoes of your message. It gives you the chance to prove beyond a shadow of a doubt that what you are sharing with people is worthy of being taken back to the classroom and used with students. It becomes the point of no return. If your PD session or event is to be effective and successful, you have to deliver in the middle.

Try these strategies for beefing up the middle of your session or event.

Action Steps

After sharing with attendees, take a break in the middle to allow participants to craft their action steps. Share several strategies with them that can have a meaningful impact in the classroom if implemented properly, and for a few minutes mid-session, allow for the planning of how to implement these strategies. "You just learned some great information about how to teach writing in your content area. Now, what actions can you take tomorrow that will help you begin to do this with your students?" Have participants write down three to five action steps and share them with someone else. The act of writing the steps down and saying them out loud will help the attendee follow through on the action steps. Encourage colleagues to take their written action steps back to their classroom and tape them to their desk or above their computer. The goal is to carry over what you learned during a PD session into actionable steps back in your classroom. If the steps are visible, attendees are more likely to make them happen.

Find an Action Steps Worksheet below:

3, 2, 1, Go!

We've already shared the importance of building reflection into professional development. Having time to think clearly about what you've learned can help you create a plan for accomplishing something based on what you just learned. Consider taking a moment in the middle to have participants quickly jot down the following:

- 3 things they've learned so far
- 2 questions they still have
- 1 way they will use what they've learned to do something differently

While this gives attendees the chance to reflect upon their learning and begin the process of applying what they've learned, you can also generate some questions to address for the second half of your professional development proceeding. Have participants write down their two questions on separate sticky notes, then stand up and place them in a central location in the room. As the facilitator, you can work these questions into the remainder of your session.

A Moment of Silence

Silence can be difficult. It can also be incredibly powerful. Use silence to drive participants into contemplation and reflection. Start by explaining the rules. Three minutes of silence. No noise. Because silence can be hard, someone may try to break the silence—a forced cough, a question, a deep sigh. Provide a gentle reminder for everyone to maintain quiet in order to give everyone time to reflect. Ask attendees to sit quietly and think about what they have learned so far. As colleagues sit silently, use several prompting questions (in a hushed tone, of course):

- What is the most important thing you've learned so far?
- How will you use this new information to help students?
- How will you use this information to alter your practice?
- What will you take away from our session today?

The act of silence can help participants really focus on what they are learning. Normally a session goes by quickly (especially if you are learning). The session may be filled with collaborative noise if participants are sharing, or the sound of the facilitator voice. Silence may be an eerie feeling in the room, but again, it can serve as a powerful tool to create introspection among colleagues.

Play PD TAG

I like to kick off my PD sessions with a round of Rock, Paper, Scissors (RPS) to get everyone actively involved. At one conference, my session was held in a small room and crowded with screaming hordes trying to prove their dominance at RPS. A person who was presenting in the room next door popped in to find out what all of the noise was and encouraged us to quiet down. Being shushed by another PD presenter? It might have been one of my crowning professional achievements.

There is something about getting attendees to actively participate during a PD session. Try getting everyone up mid-session to play a game of TAG. Not a traditional run around the room and chase down colleagues, but rather "Take And Give." Participants will stand and walk around the room to as many people as possible during a certain time frame (three to five minutes is probably a good target!). When they meet each person, they will *take* something the other person has learned so far and *give* something they have learned. It's a great way to keep everyone from being sedentary during the session. (Always keep in mind any participants who may have mobility issues, and provide an alternative option of sitting and sharing.) It provides a standing break and gives everyone a chance to reflect on their learning to that point in the session. Plus, colleagues may build some additional connection that could propel them forward in their learning.

Yes, everyone wants to focus on the kickoff and the big-bang ending, but don't sleep on the middle. The middle provides a perfect time for reflection, collaboration, and action. The middle provides an opportunity to do something different that can help educators to grow. Instead of the traditional lull that might happen mid-session, make sure you make the middle meaningful.

After all, it's all about the middle.

PD Rule #6: Look for the Obvious

Several years ago, I was organizing our district's professional development day. We had a number of great options for teachers, but I was hoping to add just a few more before the event. I reached out to a teacher well versed in classroom management and behavior strategies and asked if she wouldn't mind leading a discussion based session at the upcoming PD event. After some pleading, she agreed to lead a discussion for regular education teachers during the morning sessions, and a discussion for special education colleagues in the afternoon.

On the day of the event, I stopped by the classroom to see how the morning session was going. In the classroom, which normally housed about twenty-five students, there were nearly sixty educators crammed into the room, sitting on desks, taking up spaces on the floor, and piled onto the countertops in the classroom. There was a lively conversation about student behaviors and management strategies taking place. In the afternoon, I observed the same scene, with educators stuffed into the now overcrowded space and passionately sharing classroom management strategies that had worked for them.

During our post-event reflection, I was glad I had asked the teacher to lead a session at the last minute. While I hadn't initially considered classroom management to be a relevant topic for teachers, after the fact, it was quite obvious. Of course classroom management sessions should be included at future PD events.

We may sometimes ignore the obvious because the topics may seem self-explanatory. With classroom management, I assumed that only new teachers needed specific training or strategies. Based on the popularity of the sessions, I learned that more teachers were looking for something to help them with behaviors in the classroom.

So, rule #6: look for the obvious.

What are the glaring needs for teachers? Does a particular topic keep coming up on PD surveys? There's an obvious need for teachers. Deliver on the topic to make sure that educators are getting what they need.

Find the pain points. As we stated earlier in the book, educators love to complain! The complaints and groans usually provide more obvious clues about professional development needs. Keep your ear to the ground and listen for areas of dissatisfaction. Deliver on those obvious needs.

Look for the obvious and use it to your advantage.

Chapter 6

Planned PD Days

"Murder your darlings."

—SIR ARTHUR QUILLER-COUCH,
ON THE ART OF WRITING

We've all been there. The dreaded district PD day. Some still call it an in-service. Some try to jazz it up and call it a staff professional learning day. No matter what it is called, it has the potential to send teachers back to their classrooms motivated and inspired or overwhelmed with frustration. With how important the day is, it is surprising that in many districts, the day is planned by only one person. I've been in that position. It's incredibly difficult to plan meaningful and relevant professional learning for a large group of educators.

Everyone wants something different.

Everyone needs something different.

Everyone thinks they know exactly what the day should look like.

So, for those planning the all-important district PD day, two questions arise and bring about a number of sub-questions:

Content and learning: What can actually be accomplished in six hours?

- District initiatives?
- School-based or grade-level initiatives?
- Educator-driven discussions and conversations?
- Technology training?
- State-mandated training?

Structure and logistics: How do we accomplish it?

- How can we include educator choice or agency?
- Large groups or small groups?
- Shorter or longer sessions?
- How do we build in reflection and discussion time?

While one person can usually answer these questions, it typically becomes a more productive use of time when multiple stakeholders have a chance to answer the questions. Planning the entire day should not be the sole responsibility of one person or even two people. It should fall to a committed group of educators, those in formal leadership positions (both district- and school-based administrators) and those occupying informal leadership positions (teacher leaders, technology facilitators, PD content providers, and others). I have found that the best district-wide PD days all have one thing in common. The goals, planning, and outcomes all come from the input of multiple stakeholders—the ROGUE Leaders, if you will.

Find your ROGUE friends. In some cases, you may even need to find your ROGUE enemies. Find those who will bring a different perspective to the PD planning process. Find someone who brings different PD needs or is seeking a different outcome. When multiple perspectives, viewpoints, and attitudes are brought to the PD planning stage, it can help to make that dreaded district PD day diverge into something more beautiful, more functional, and more productive. Plan together. Make it meaningful. Make it relevant. It's no longer the *dreaded* district PD day, because it doesn't have to be that way.

The Plight of the Professional Professional Development Planner

It is rather difficult to be in charge of professional development. I served in a district role in charge of PD for several years, and I can assure you, it is a thankless position.

Let's break it down.

I was in charge of helping 350 instructional staff members participate in exactly the right PD to help them become better educators. Each of those people has different wants and needs. Keep in mind that this group includes the kindergarten art teacher, the middle school art teacher, a speech teacher, an occupational therapist, fourteen different third-grade teachers, and a counselor who serves everyone from preschool through sixth grade, among many others with very specific needs. To say the needs are diverse is a slight bit of distortion.

Each of those 350 staff members work in five different buildings with five completely different schedules. It doesn't work to say: Can everyone attend this meeting at 4 p.m. today? The answer is always a resounding nope. In fact, the management of the timing, scheduling, and logistics that go into making professional development work often becomes the aspect that will make the professional PD planner throw up their hands and throw in the towel. Giving up is considered a better option than trying to make it work.

Oh, yeah—important side note: Each of those five buildings has a completely different culture, atmosphere, and environment, with a different leader who shapes and molds that culture. Some of the leaders agree with each other about what should be done with the PD time, and some do not. In fact, the disagreement likely occurs in an especially argumentative manner and tone. Some leaders just don't cherish collaboration like the rest of us. Trying to project a consistent message can be a wee bit challenging. Aligning multiple leaders and buildings on PD day can be a daunting proposition that causes the weak to jump ship at the first sign of distress.

The day finally arrives in early March: a district-wide PD day, in which all staff from all buildings gather in one place to learn together. There are also four to five state and county mandated training sessions that need to take place. The student services department wants a group to be recertified in CPR. All upper-grade teachers need to receive training on the new state-standardized testing system. Building initiatives abound. District programs and training are a must, and before you know it, the day is gone.

Once you come up with a schedule to accommodate all the mandated programs, there is no additional time for any staff members' individual learning needs. You email out the schedule, then resend it after you realize there is another mandated training that needs to take place that the Director of Other Tasks and Remover of Joy (probably an unofficial title) just mentioned to you. The teachers end up with multiple copies of a list of places to go and training to do that doesn't reflect what they actually need.

And the person who is seen as bad at their job is the *professional* professional development planner. What a difficult position to be in . . .

On the other hand, if the PD planner is amazing at their job and can convince the teachers to take charge of their own professional development, then that person minimizes their own impact.

So, the question becomes:

How do we get teachers to engage in developing themselves?

The ultimate theoretical goal should be to eliminate those who plan professional development. It's not about actually trying to eliminate the position, but rather to minimize the responsibility that one person has for the PD needs of everyone else. I've already written about some other ways to share the responsibility for PD. We know that it can't just be a one-person show. But we have to ensure that district PD days capture the power of connection that effective PD can deliver. We have to ensure that PD continues to be purposeful and consequential for everyone. In short, we want to create an atmosphere where teachers want to attend district PD days rather than have that deep-in-their gut feeling of dread about them.

Let's examine a school-based PD day for a moment. On these days, students stay home and teachers continue to learn. This system can actually tell us a great deal about our instructional program as well as our professional development design. We can ask two questions that tell us everything we need to know:

1. Are students excited to be home or are they sad to be missing school?
2. Are educators excited to be at PD or do they take the day off?

We want students who are running to get back into school because of the learning experiences that exist there. Likewise, we want educators to be running through the door because they are excited about the learning opportunities that are available on a school-provided PD day.

What if we killed two birds with one stone and gave teachers the chance to learn alongside students on PD days? Is it something that could work? If we think about our ultimate goal of improving student learning outcomes with our professional development program, then we know that involving students in the process can only help. We can gain valuable insight about our practices from our actual end users. We can help students gain leadership experience and help both teachers and students continue to learn and grow together.

Win. Win.

Try these approaches to involve students in your district PD days:

Student-Led Feedback Loops

Think whole-group and small-group discussion about learning with teachers *and* students. Let students share their opinions about school by asking questions like these:

- What do you like about school?
- What do you dislike about school?
- What part(s) of school can be improved?
- What should we keep? What should we get rid of?
- If you were in charge of school, what would you do differently?

Once students feel comfortable sharing in this type of setting, use the feedback to solve problems and create meaningful change in how things are done. We have created a student advisory committee at our elementary school made up of a group of second- through fifth-graders. You haven't really considered what school is until you've seen it through the eyes of an elementary-aged kid. Gather student feedback. Have teachers and students talk through what works and what doesn't. Explain to students the "why" behind certain actions or systems. Come to mutual understandings and make changes where necessary and possible.

Student-Led "Appy" Hour or Tech Speed Dating

Students are always a step ahead of us when it comes to technology. During virtual learning, students quickly figured out that they could loop a short video of themselves looking like they were paying attention and use it as their background. When a teacher glanced at the screen, it appeared as if the student was listening attentively and always nodding (somewhat aggressively!) in agreement. This was a shortcut that students mastered quickly before teachers had fully figured out the operation of online video platforms that were thrust upon them. The lesson: kids are smart and can be better at technology than the adults. How do we harness this power (and sometimes evil genius!)?

Let students get involved in PD days by sharing out the latest and greatest technology tips, tricks, and hacks that they have figured out. Try a student-led "Appy" Hour. Students share a brief two-minute sales pitch about what they will help teachers learn. After each student shares their pitch, teachers choose which tech platform, resource, tool, or strategy they'd like to learn more about. Students must research and learn about the platforms they will be using at school, gaining skills in presenting and leading, while teachers obtain a better understanding of the tools they are using with students. More importantly, they get a glimpse into *how* students are using them.

One of the most successful student-led Appy Hours that I witnessed featured a group of third-grade students showing teachers how to use YouTube. The students had started their own YouTube channel and were uploading and sharing videos about a variety of video games they played. They showed teachers how to start a YouTube channel, trim videos, and upload them to the channel. Teachers learned some how-to logistics but also saw how students were using the tech tool. Teachers came away with a new sense of what was possible by using YouTube, instead of immediately dismissing it as a potentially dangerous tool.

Modify the activity to expose colleagues to more tools. Student-led Tech Speed Dating can work in much the same way. Each student involved can share about a different tool, resource, or strategy and present short three-to-five-minute presentations to help teachers learn. Teachers then jump from student to student to learn about each of the different resources. This type of collaborative learning can help improve relationships and create meaningful connections.

Genius Hour for Teachers and Students

English (as the class was called then) was my least favorite class because I didn't like to read or write (or so I thought at the time). I would even go so far as to say I hated English class. So it was a weird occurrence when I came to join an after-school club known as the Writing Irish. (Our school teams were nicknamed the Fighting Irish.) I joined because one of my friends was joining. He was joining because his older sister happened to be a part of the club and could drive him home. I then became part of the package deal and got dropped off each Tuesday afternoon as well.

This ended up being one of the best experiences of my high school years. The club was responsible for publishing a literary journal at the end of the year that featured the writing and artwork of students. In my first couple of years participating I would work closely with the student editor in chief and two teachers who were responsible for overseeing the project. It was great to work collaboratively with teachers to make decisions about what the end product would eventually look like. As part of the team, we would decide layout, text placement, order, and artwork choice to try to capture certain moods within the journal.

Little did I know that many of the skills I learned working with my teachers and classmates on the journal would come to serve me well later in life, when I learned that I actually do, in fact, enjoy writing and publishing. In my senior year, I was fortunate to have the experience of serving as coeditor in chief with my friend and another classmate (we called ourselves the Triumvirate!), and it gave me a new perspective on the possibility of creative collaboration between students and teachers.

Something I could never have predicted was that this was an early version of what might come to be known as a Genius Hour project. (Genius Hour is a period of time each week for students to work on something that they are passionate about outside of the standard curriculum.) I was working on something I was passionate about. The teachers were working on something they were passionate about. And in the end, we were able to produce a product we could all be proud of.

A Genius Hour collaboration can be an awesome way for educators and students to learn together. It could be a literary journal. Maybe it's a shared podcast between teacher and student that helps other educators learn about the student perspective. Students and teachers could work together to create new project-based assessments that are more equitable than standardized assessments. There is power in collaboration with students. I think about the learning that takes place when a teacher models the writing process for their second-grade students. A shared writing piece helps everyone learn.

How amazing would it be to create a shared Genius Hour for teachers and students on your next PD day? What would they learn? What would they produce? What would they come up with that would be amazing for everyone involved? We could ask twenty more questions about what might become of such a project, but the possibilities are endless. Create your own Student/Teacher Genius Hour. See what magic can happen. Be sure to share because the rest of us will want to see what it can become!

Five Ways to Use Feedback to Plan PD

PD surveys: Ask colleagues to complete a survey. What is working? What is not working? What topics or formats would educators like to see? Use Google Forms to capture the survey data easily. If you are seeking truly honest data, have educators take the survey anonymously. The data you receive can provide a valuable glimpse into educator attitudes toward professional development. Use the survey results to assist with PD design, as well as to help change the culture surrounding professional development. Anonymous survey results can quickly show you if you have a PD problem.

Meta PD: PD about PD. Take twenty minutes at your next staff meeting to discuss and plan your next PD opportunities. Ask how colleagues learn best, what can be done to improve professional learning, and how to ensure that PD is meaningful and relevant for everyone involved. Taking just a few minutes to plan PD with all stakeholders ensures that each educator's voice is heard during the PD process.

Post-PD reflection: Usually, we ask teachers what they learned after a PD session. Instead, focus on application. Change your question to ask: "How will you apply this learning with your students?" Ask adult learners to take pictures of the application of professional development and share them with colleagues. Reflection and sharing with colleagues can extend the professional development process and allow educators to continue their learning.

Work out the kinks first: Trying new strategies or methods of instruction? Let certain teachers try out something first and figure out the pros and cons before introducing the idea to other teachers. Perfect the method(s) in a controlled environment and share feedback from piloting teachers with colleagues. A sound pilot can help determine whether a new initiative is worth the effort before facing the uphill climb of complete implementation.

Actual PD improvements: One of the worst things an educator can do is ask for feedback, then never use it. Gather feedback, reflect on it, and make changes that improve the product. Professional development should be constantly evolving. Feedback must be a part of your process for driving professional development. It has to be used to determine strengths and weaknesses and made an integral part of planning PD sessions.

Addition by Subtraction

Because district-wide professional development time is so scarce, the PD planners out there often try to cram as much as possible into the day. A typical planned district PD day might look something like this:

8:00–8:30: Coffee/Introductions

8:30–9:00: Keynote Speaker

9:05–9:55: Session #1

10:00–10:50: Session #2

10:55–11:45: Session #3

11:45–12:45: Lunch

12:45–1:35: Session #4

1:40–2:30: Session #5

2:35–3:25: Session #6

3:25–3:40: Final Remarks

As you can see, this is a jam-packed day in which there isn't much room to breathe. Educators are shuffled from one session to another with only minimal time in between each session to reflect on learning. If this is what a typical PD day looks like in your setting, I can guarantee only two things:

1. Educators will feel a sense of exhaustion at the end of this day.
2. Educators will feel overwhelmed when they try to transfer any of their learning to the classroom with students.

For years, we looked at the normal high school schedule of shuffling students from one forty-five-minute class to another, cramming eight periods into a day as the gold standard of instruction. In fact, many high schools (and middle schools, and even elementary schools to a certain extent!) still operate under this assumption. It's no surprise that PD planners gravitate toward the same type of schedule. The thinking goes that if we stuff as many sessions into the day, then we will find some sort of success. Six hours of PD. Six different sessions.

Teachers will be able to learn at least one thing! For the math teachers (and gamblers) reading, we are simply playing the percentages.

Some high schools have figured out that the typical period-one-to-eight model doesn't work as well as we initially thought. These schools use a block schedule, which is more aligned to what we might see at a college level. Yet we still try to play the percentages and cram as much as possible into our PD days.

Let's go back to our original PD day schedule and see if we can't add to the day by subtracting. Let's take some things off the plate in order to give educators more time to breathe and, more importantly, to reflect.

8:00–8:30: Coffee/Introductions

8:30–9:00: ~~Keynote Speaker~~

9:05–9:55: Session #1

10:00–10:50: Session #2

10:55–11:45: Session #3

11:45–12:45: Lunch

12:45–1:35: Session #4

1:40–2:30: ~~Session #5~~

2:35–3:25: ~~Session #6~~

3:25–3:40: ~~Final Remarks~~

Now that we've eliminated a few things, let's adjust the schedule to provide more time for reflection and collaboration.

8:00–8:30: Coffee/Introductions

8:45–9:45: Session #1

9:45–10:15: Reflection/Collaboration Time

10:15–11:15: Session #2

11:15–11:45: Reflection/Collaboration Time

11:45–12:45: Lunch

12:45–1:45: Session #3

1:45–2:15: Reflection/Collaboration Time

2:15–3:15: Session #4

3:15–3:45: Reflection/Collaboration Time

This schedule remains mostly the same as the original schedule. It is roughly the same amount of time, still provides for an hour-long lunch period, and even extends each session from forty-five minutes to one hour. Plus, the updated schedule allows for two hours of reflection and collaboration for educators. Our instincts tell us that we want to pack as much as possible into a PD day. We want to give teachers every chance to learn something they can take back to the classroom for their students. But sometimes, we have to add to the day by taking away. It will seem foreign at first, as though you are taking a step back. But what you will quickly realize is that teachers will appreciate the room to breathe. They will take advantage of the reflection and collaboration time as well.

Remember that some of the best moments from a district PD day come in the hallway when two educators who don't normally get to meet with each other come together and share something they just learned. "If you get the chance, you should check out the session on 360-degree math. I think it would be something you and your students would love!" The gauntlet has been thrown down, and another educator is now intrigued by an idea. Once an idea is shared, there is no telling where that idea can take you. Building in reflection and collaboration time encourages conversations and allows good ideas (and good PD) to spread among colleagues in a district.

PD Operations and Logistics

One of the greatest difficulties professional development planners face is logistics. It can be an onerous task to try to meet everyone's needs at the same time. You need to worry about space and physical locations. You have to take into account timing and schedules. You need to plan for multiple sessions that address a plethora of mandates, wants, needs, and preferences. Dealing with professional development operations can cause major headaches.

And yet someone needs to be in charge.

Here are some considerations to think about when dealing with logistics and PD ops:

Get formal help: You won't be able to do it alone. Trust me. I tried early on. You will need help. I've found that when planning, you need some key figures involved in order to make your PD sessions go off without a hitch. You will need someone to support logistics who can get the job done no matter what the task. I've been fortunate to work with some amazing administrative assistants during my time in education. They always know everything and have a way of knowing what I'm thinking even before I'm thinking it. You will need someone like this to support the thousand small details so that nothing slips through the cracks. Consider relying on a trusted team. Someone can plan the big-picture details. Someone can be responsible for all the small details. Someone can manage the group so that everything is coordinated on the day of the event. Running an efficient and meaningful PD event cannot be accomplished by one person alone. Find your team and let them help to ensure it runs smoothly.

Speaking of help, *involve your tech team.* You might plan for months to ensure that your PD event is perfect, and on the day of, there is no doubt you will find a simple technology glitch can bring the whole thing crashing down. Involve your tech team early to make sure you are doing things the right way so as not to cause problems later on. When a tech issue does arise on the day of the event, have your tech team around to troubleshoot and come to your rescue. Again, I've been fortunate to work with strong technology departments throughout my career. They are the unsung heroes of PD operations.

Technology failures and glitches should be an expected function of a PD event. I've never been a part of a PD day in which we didn't experience some type of technology problem. I'm glad I always had our tech experts there to back me up.

Consider your backup plan: Issues will certainly emerge as your PD event kicks off. A scheduled presenter may be late or a no-show. Technology may not work. The power will go out. If something can go wrong, it will. The key is having a backup contingency ready to go when things go south. Come up with a plan B. Have plans C and D ready to go. (Keep in mind that there are twenty-six letters in the alphabet!) Rely on others to help you here. Know who your go-to presenters will be in the case of a no-show. As discussed, have your brilliant tech team ready and willing to step in when there is a WiFi issue or when a presenter has compatibility problems with their device. A good PD planner always has multiple options in case something doesn't work. I once had the power go out right before the first session of a PD day. All the presenters who had been ready to share via technology were suddenly grounded. After several attempts to get the power up and running, our plan B was natural sunlight and in-depth conversation about our planned topics. The first session still managed to be productive, as teachers engaged in discussions. We managed to get power back shortly before the second session was about to begin, and we were able to make the best of the situation. Always consider your backup plan!

Consider your space (and facilities): If you are planning a large-scale event, you will definitely need to give major consideration to the facilities that you will be using. Multiple presenters and sessions will require the use of many rooms. Each room will need to be equipped with the appropriate technology for presenters. Some presenters may prefer a more open space and not have a need for technology. The wants, preferences, and needs of those delivering PD should drive your considerations for the learning spaces you will be using. Also keep in mind that if you are hosting a district-wide event, you need to consider the parking available for all staff. I've been to a district-wide event that barely had enough parking for attendees. The first twenty minutes of the afternoon session was spent by many trying to find a parking spot as they returned from lunch. Be sure to think clearly about what your presenters and audience want and need in their learning spaces. Use facilities that will comfortably host all of your attendees. If you don't pay enough attention to your learning spaces and facility usage, your PD event could suffer immensely.

Plan for the long term: If you are trying to plan a PD event for colleagues or staff, you will focus a great deal of energy on making the event meaningful, productive, and successful. Just know that a short time later, you will need to provide follow-up PD or other opportunities for staff to engage in self-directed learning. Don't ever be short-sighted in your professional development planning. Consider an overall plan for what you want to accomplish with an in-depth professional learning program. Ask yourself a series of questions to start: What should PD look like for the next month? The next six months? The next year? The next two years? The next five years? Thinking about a single PD event in the context of a five-year professional development plan will allow you to make more clear decisions in your planning. Creating a consistent, well-designed professional development program is not built on a single PD session or event alone. You must give critical thought to what PD should look like over the long term.

Considering everything we've discussed in this chapter, how do you ultimately improve your PD days? Follow these simple steps to make your district PD day better!

Murder your darlings: Take a look at the schedule for your last district PD day. While it may be difficult, take the advice of Sir Arthur Quiller-Couch and "murder your darlings." While this advice is often given to writers during the revision process, suggesting that they not get so attached to an element of their writing that they can't eliminate it for the betterment of the final piece, it also works well when thinking about our PD days. Look at the previous schedule and eliminate anything that is not directly having a great impact on professional growth and student learning outcomes. It might mean getting rid of that wonderful keynote speaker. It might mean limiting the number of minutes that talking heads and ceremonial speakers (from the central office and the board of education) take from the day. It might involve eliminating a number of sessions that have been happening for years but ceased being relevant fifteen years ago. Simply put, get rid of anything that is not making the day fundamentally better.

Try a little R&R: The day should be about learning, but you also need to build in time for **Reflection and Reciprocity**. Educators learn from one another. When there is a give-and-take mentality present during your PD day, people will be excited to learn from others, but also primed to share with others. Create a Give & Take Board on your next PD day to promote reflection and reciprocity. The idea is simple. A bulletin board, poster board, or chart paper can be set up to encourage teachers to reflect upon their learning. Use sticky notes to allow educators to share something they learned about—a website, strategy, or resource. After posting something on the Give & Take board, each teacher has the opportunity to take a sticky note as well. This helps to spread ideas! Encourage participants to write their email address on the sticky note as well. This means that educators can connect after the PD day to continue to collaborate and learn from each other.

Don't forget your VCR: A few years ago, Principal Jon Craig, who was then an instructional coach, shared an idea of how he plans district PD days. He makes sure that he doesn't forget his VCR—**Voice, Choice, and Relevance**. It's a simple acronym that can help you remember exactly what needs to be included in any district PD day:

Voice: Provide opportunities for educators to share their voice. Start with surveys before the event to find out exactly what teachers are looking for during the event. Use the surveys to help you plan and create a day that is meaningful for everyone involved. Provide a structure for gathering post-event feedback as well. Use an online post-event survey or gather pros and cons through Google Forms. This valuable information can help you constantly improve professional development days in your setting. Ensure that educators have a voice in how the day looks and feels!

Choice: Build in chances for choice throughout the day. Sessions can be offered multiple times during the day to give teachers the chance to participate as they see fit. A wide variety of offerings should be planned to address a wide variety of wants and needs for educators. Also, build in different types of learning opportunities. Participants may want to choose whatever type of session works best for them—discussion-based, interactive, lecture, participatory, hands-on, inquiry-based, etc. Choice should be an integral part of the day.

Relevance: Make sure that the day features chances for educators to take part in relevant content. Consider new initiatives and implementations in which teachers are seeking support. Have technology leaders present new and updated technology resources that can help teachers immediately in the classroom. While trendy buzzwords and programs can be appealing, focus on sessions that provide usable content. Remember that relevance doesn't mean "shiny and new"; it means that teachers will be able to take it back to their classrooms in order to improve student learning outcomes.

Learn more about VCR from Jon's video for 4OCF Summer Camp:

To Lunch or Not to Lunch? That Is the Question

On most days as an educator, you are rushing through your lunch with six other things on your plate that need to get done. You may have thirty or forty minutes to eat, but you also have to drop your students off at the cafeteria, use the bathroom for the first time since 7 a.m., make copies, and hand in important paperwork to the main office. It exists as a hurried frenzy of task completion and scarfing down what you consider a meal. If you eat a meal at all. I sometimes look up at the clock to realize it's 4:15 p.m. and I haven't eaten my lunch. Educator lunch is simply not an enjoyable time.

Unless it's lunch on a PD day. There is no rushing. There are no copies to be made. There may be important paperwork to hand in, but it can wait. The lunch hour (or half hour or forty-five minutes) is often one of the best parts of any PD experience. First of all, most people love food and eating. Secondly, most people love sharing a normally paced meal among good company while enjoying good conversation.

I've seen some districts that eliminate a lunch hour on PD days. The thinking here is that the day ends a little earlier, and the time allotted for lunch is seen as superfluous to the day.

I've also seen districts who provide an open lunch hour for staff on a PD day during which teachers can leave campus and go to a local restaurant to eat or bring their lunch back.

While you may be able to strike a balance for what works in your setting, I'd like to advocate for a particular strategy here. First and foremost, do *not* eliminate the lunch hour on PD day. It provides a great opportunity for colleagues to share time together. Secondly, don't skimp and shorten the lunch hour. Make it an actual hour. Not forty-five minutes. Not thirty minutes. Give everyone the time needed to actually digest a meal and also share in a conversation with like-minded individuals (for a change)!

The best way to make lunch a meaningful part of the day is to offer *free* lunch. That's right. You heard it correctly. The best way to meaningful PD is a *free* meal. I'm sure this idea sounds vaguely familiar. If it does, that's because I wrote about it in the first book. But guess what? It still works. It will always work.

A few years ago, during a district-wide PD day, we were able to partner with local restaurants to provide a pizza and salad lunch for more than 300 staff members. Teachers had the option to go out during the lunch hour if they wanted, but they didn't need to because we had all the food set up right in the cafeteria. Some teachers who were not fans of pizza or salad (what?!?) brown-bagged their own lunch. The beauty of this setup was that most staff members stayed in the large cafeteria, grabbed some food, and enjoyed lunch and conversation with their colleagues. There was laughter. There was sharing. There was reflection. It was meaningful conversation. There was a hum of excitement in the air. No one felt rushed to go out and get food, then have to be back in time for the afternoon sessions. Some staff members who preferred a quieter setting went back to a classroom with a few colleagues to share and connect. The staff members simply enjoyed the lunch hour.

The one thing I noticed as I walked around during lunch and checked in with people was that lunch conversations focused on the learning that had taken place in the morning ("I learned this really simple strategy for building a culture of writing in my classroom"). It also gave educators a chance to think about what their afternoon looked like ("I loved the session on yoga in the classroom. You should check it out this afternoon"). The lunchtime discussions gravitated toward the learning that was taking place. And that's the best we can ask for.

So, to recap:

Keep lunch hour on PD day. An hour. Not fifty-five minutes. Not forty minutes. One full hour.

Provide lunch for those who are interested. Partner with local restaurants to provide pizza (it's super easy!) or find a place that does boxed lunches and delivers!

Leave options open. Some can brown-bag their own lunch (because of dietary needs). Some will choose to eat in a large gathering area like the cafeteria. Some will choose to go back to a classroom. It doesn't matter where people eat, so long as it's enjoyable.

Most of all, let educators enjoy lunch for a change. They don't get to do this very often. It makes the entire day better!

Lunch provides the perfect opportunity for teachers to share their learning. While they are enjoying the time, they will also be sharing, collaborating, and connecting. It's a great thing!

The District PD Day. It can be an experience teachers dread or it can be an experience educators can't wait to take part in. There are simple fixes that can help make the day an adventure that everyone will look forward to. Invite students to participate. Add by subtracting. Take away any parts that are not helping to improve the day. Build in time for reflection, conversation, and collaboration. Honor teacher voice. Don't let colleagues be held captive any longer by the dreaded district PD day. Make it a day everyone will remember. More importantly, make it a day where educators learn how to improve their practice and grow as professionals!

ROGUE Leader Reflections

PD Keys

- District-wide PD should be created with input from a wide variety of stakeholders. Consider the viewpoints from formal and informal leaders, teachers, instructional and technology coaches, and students. Don't forget the opinions of students!
- Add to professional development by subtracting. Rather than a jam-packed, nonstop PD day, give educators the chance to breathe and reflect upon their learning.
- Some of the best PD happens when teachers have the chance to meet and talk to each other. Build discussion and sharing time into district-wide PD events.

A Question to Ponder

What do you dread about your district-wide PD opportunities and how can you build a better PD day for yourself and your colleagues?

PD Checkpoint #6: This Is Jeopardy!

For a half hour each day, you're reminded that the most important things you need to learn must be phrased in the form of a question. Or rather: What are the most important things I learned today?

Jeopardy! is a fascinating TV show for many. The draw is our obsession with learning and knowledge. Jot down some topics you would like to learn more about in the next six months. Don't forget to list everything in the form of a question!

1. _____

2. _____

3. _____

4. _____

5. _____

6. _____

7. _____

Go through your list and decide which is most important right away. Find a way to incorporate your priority into an upcoming PD session.

PD Rule #7: Address Wants and Needs (and Everything in Between!)

Professional development often addresses deficits. Consideration is given to areas where teachers are considered to be "weak" or where teachers need to sharpen their skills. Deficit thinking in the area of PD can lead to poor decision-making. One-and-done workshops are aimed at addressing the deficits of teachers. A short-term fix might be implemented and teachers trained without looking at the root cause of problems.

As is also the case in our work with students, if we only focus on deficits, we miss other parts that make up the learner. If we only focus on the perceived weakness of a learner in reading, we might miss that she is an amazing painter. If we hone in on the struggling math skills of a learner, we might not see the tremendous writer that lies beneath.

PD, like our work with students, has to work the same way. Yes, sometimes we need to address a deficit in order to help teachers grow as learners. But we must also address wants in addition to needs. Providing PD choices that allow for educator interests as well as needs helps to round out our professional development offerings.

We need sessions that help teachers grow in areas of strength, too. How can that awesome math teacher down the hall take it to the next level? How does a teacher who's interested in photography bring that passion into the classroom? How can we help teachers incorporate creativity practices in the classroom?

So let's abide by rule #7: address wants *and* needs (and everything in between)!

Let's boost confidence for our colleagues. Let's create PD that addresses the areas our colleagues excel at. Let's address areas in which teachers *need* help. Let's pinpoint topics in which teachers *want* help.

Just as we say with students, when we talk about our adult colleagues, let's focus on the whole learner!

Chapter 7

Staff Well-Being

"Self-care is giving the world the best
of you, not what's left of you."

—KATIE REED, *THE BORDERLINE BLOG*

It started with a student sent to the office. He was not a regular visitor to the office, and I could see the frustration on his face. I questioned him about why he was sent to the office. His teacher was normally apt to handle any issues in her classroom before taking the extreme measure of involving me. In fact, her class was particularly well managed and, for the most part, so engaged in learning that they didn't have time to get into trouble. He let out an incredible sigh of exasperation and followed it with a response I often hear from students when they are sent to the office: "I don't even know what I did."

Over the years, I've gotten stronger at reading kids, and I recognized from his frustration that he was telling the truth. He wasn't quite sure what had gotten him sent to the office in the first place. And so we had a conversation. I asked what had happened right before he was sent down. He explained that all he did was simply ask a friend a question, but that his teacher had been correcting the entire class all morning, and when she heard him talk, she immediately sent him to the office. I asked the student to wait a few minutes in the office while I went and spoke with his teacher.

As soon as she saw me come to the classroom, she knew. She was frustrated and aggravated. "I'm sorry, Rich. They haven't been listening all morning, and I know I shouldn't have sent him down, but I just couldn't take it anymore!"

At that point in the year, it was a very familiar feeling.

Exhaustion. Frustration. Lack of motivation. It was all wrapped up in the expressions of those I saw in the building each day. Students were anxious and rambunctious. And teachers were more easily losing their cool. It was easy to recognize that everyone—staff and students alike—were stressed beyond their limits.

So I did what any administrator would do. I made sure to send an email to remind the staff about our upcoming staff meeting on Thursday.

I did add one caveat, though, in my email: "Make sure that you wear comfortable clothing. We will be participating in a physical activity." Several staff members came and asked the obvious questions:

- What do you mean by comfortable clothing?
- How comfortable can I be?

And finally, the questions I heard often:

- What are we really going to be doing at our staff meeting?
- Why don't you just tell us?

I tried to vaguely answer the questions so as not to ruin the surprise.

Prior to my reminder email, I had been planning a detailed agenda for our monthly staff meeting. This one, even by my standards, was pretty tame. I actually had some business that needed to be conducted at the meeting, and so I had planned to address the required items and then move quickly into modeling instructional practices.

But after I continued to experience the frustration and exhaustion from students and staff, I decided to scrap the meeting. It probably would have been OK to send out an email that read:

Good afternoon, everyone. I recognize that everyone could use a break, so we will not be having our staff meeting as scheduled this week.

Instead, I decided to host a staff meeting and give all of our teachers a chance to blow off some steam. I found our physical education teacher and mentioned my idea to him. He, as always, was ready to run with it. We quickly planned a couple of activities. First, Human Hungry Hungry Hippos. Neither of us had any experience with this game, but we had seen some really exciting videos online, so we decided to give it a shot. If that went well, we would continue with it. If not, we planned on falling back on a classic: a game of dodgeball.

On the day of the staff meeting, teachers were excited to find out what we'd be doing during the after-school staff meeting. I hoped that our PE colleague hadn't spilled the beans, and I tried to keep it under wraps throughout the day. At 3:45, we gathered in the gym, and I explained that everyone had been working way too hard and that we needed a moment to breathe (or, in this case, play Human Hungry Hungry Hippos)! My colleagues weren't quite sure what to make of this game, but they energetically gave their all. After a few rounds, I offered the choice of sticking with the game or finishing up with a round of dodgeball before we called it a day.

The group was resolute in its decision to start a dodgeball game. We quickly lined up the dodgeballs and split into two teams. When the whistle blew, both teams took on an intensity I hadn't seen since some backyard football games when I was thirteen. The intensity level was high. Dodgeballs rocketed across the gym. Players dove to save teammates. Colleagues who were normally friendly threw the balls with all their might to try to get others out. I was afraid that someone was going to get hurt.

On my drive home from school that night, I felt like teachers were able to let go, if only for a little while. It wasn't until I showed up at school the next morning that I noticed the difference in the atmosphere in the building. My colleagues seemed loose. They seemed free. They seemed like they had a forty-pound weight lifted off their shoulders. And the other group in the building I noticed the difference in was the students. To this day, it is one of the greatest staff meetings I've ever been a part of.

So knowing how successful this type of meeting can be, why don't we have more staff-meeting dodgeball games? The simple answer is that we usually don't have enough time. Even as a current school administrator, I find it difficult to manage everything that needs to get done during our "PD time" and trying to dedicate time to teachers' social-emotional well-being. Between mandated information, curriculum programs and updates, professional learning communities, and other professional growth opportunities, our time is in short supply.

However, we all see the teacher retention rates and know that teacher burnout is a real thing. Desiree Carver-Thomas and Linda Darling-Hammond reveal in their Learning Policy Institute report "Teacher Turnover: Why It Matters and What We Can Do About It" that the annual attrition rate among teachers nationally is 8 percent. We continue to place more responsibilities and burdens on teachers with less support and understanding about their own well-being. The teacher-as-martyr narrative is often used to continue to increase what we expect of teachers, and for many, it has an impact that can significantly shorten or end teaching careers.

What can we do about it? We first need to realize that burnout is a real thing. We need to start by dedicating some of our precious time to focusing on teacher health and well-being. We need to help educators strike more of a work-life balance. We need to let teachers know that it's OK to take care of yourself first. As they tell you during those important airplane demonstrations (that no one pays attention to!), you need to put on your oxygen mask before you are able to help anyone else with their oxygen mask.

Try these strategies and activities to ensure that you are tending to health and well-being during PD sessions:

Self-Care Is A Skill to Be Taught!

One of the reasons educators may worry about others first is that self-care doesn't always come naturally. In addition to taking care of and providing support for their students, they may also be taking care of their family at home. Some teachers may be overwhelmed and struggle to keep their head above water, especially with the ever-increasing list of tasks, duties, and responsibilities that we ask of them. Not wanting to ask for help can cause a teacher to burn out quickly. As colleagues and ROGUE Leaders, we need to recognize this and provide support for those who need to allow themselves some time for self-care. How can we support our colleagues in taking better care of themselves?

Try hosting a self-care session for colleagues. Model strategies for teachers that will help them to take better care of themselves. Discuss ways they can minimize workload or become more efficient and productive in fewer minutes during the week. Show easier ways to do things, like batching lesson plans or eliminating certain activities that require an inordinate amount of copies. Any time that you can save teachers is time that can be spent on self-care.

Provide a self-care activity that can help to bring some peace of mind to teachers. In a previous district, some of my colleagues created a choice-based self-care session, where teachers (and administrators!) could choose between three options: a seminar session on healthy cooking and healthy meals, a yoga activity period, or a one-word focus session. I joined in the latter session, where we focused on choosing our one word to focus on for the second half of the school year, then painted and decorated a small glass candle holder to represent our chosen word. It was one of the most relaxing PD sessions I've ever experienced.

Self-Care Strategy: *Try a painting party!* When you feel like you need a moment of tranquility, have you ever tried painting a picture? It can be very calming and relaxing. I've seen ROGUE Leaders set up painting parties in which an instructor (it could be a district art teacher!) shows teachers how to paint a particular picture or scene step by step. Everyone can focus on something other than education and have some fun in the process while walking away with a cool painting to decorate their classroom or home!

Sometimes, the Best PD Is No PD!

There comes a time when you just need a break. Shut it down on Saturday and Sunday. No weekend edcamps. No CoffeeEDU. No reading blogs or checking out Pinterest for lesson ideas. Log off your email. Remove the shortcut from your phone. Don't think about doing lesson plans. (Find another way to streamline your planning.) Focus on other things that you love! Give yourself the necessary grace to enjoy your time away from students and school. Remember, you need to focus on yourself first. Build in the self-care habits that will ultimately help you be a better educator. The break from everything school will make PD more meaningful when you finally go back to it!

Push Pause on PD!

Brian Kulak, a fellow principal in New Jersey, was responsible for planning his district's professional development program a few years ago. When he noticed mid-year that staff were completely stressed out and overwhelmed by the amount of district initiatives, he made the simple decision to push pause on PD! The decision was made to scrap the plans for an upcoming PD day and instead give time back to teachers to take care of themselves.

A bingo card was created with a number of different activities that staff could take part in. Staff was asked to complete five in a row on the bingo card. Activities included yoga, taking an outdoor stroll, working on unfinished projects, Ping-Pong, and basketball. Each teacher had the choice to do what they wanted or needed to do in order to de-stress. Pressing pause on the traditional planned PD initiatives gave teachers a chance to breathe, and Brian recognized the power in letting teachers step away from the initiative fatigue they were feeling. After he witnessed the aftermath of the stress-relief day, Brian realized that staff were finally able to smile for the first time in a long time.

While teachers used their free time to relax and recharge, administrators in the district locked themselves in their offices and committed to writing thank-you notes to each staff member. When the day was complete and staff returned to their classrooms or offices, each of them found a handwritten note of gratitude from one of the administrators.

Self-Care Strategy: *When you don't have time, make time.* Educators are traditionally terrible at making sure that they take time for self-care. Students come first. Families come first. Everyone else comes first. Instead of trying to find time for self-care, make time. If you are an administrator or facilitator in charge of the professional learning schedule, build in time for self-care. Once-a-week walking club? Perfect. Weekly basketball game? You bet. Monthly Ping-Pong competition? Why not. Yoga sessions? Sure. Find time. Make time. Take care of yourself first.

Hear more about the stress-relief day strategy from Brian himself:

Connections can be healthy . . .

If the growth, learning, and development offered by good PD isn't enough, maybe it's because for many PD is about the camaraderie. It's about the ability to connect with others. Yes, to learn from them, but more importantly to establish human connection. So many are able to gain from professional development in which they are able to meet and connect with other like-minded educators. Sometimes, it's difficult to connect with someone in your physical setting or location. Sometimes, it's hard to find time to connect. Sometimes, you can't find those who will challenge your thinking.

It's time that you find your sounding board and accomplice(s). The person (or people) who will help you grow to your fullest potential. Try these strategies for building connections to help you grow into a better educator.

PD pen pals: Sometimes, it can be hard to find the person that complements you as a teacher and helps you to grow each day. I've been fortunate in that I've run into several of those people throughout my career, people who have not only challenged my thinking, but also helped me to expand and stretch beyond my comfort zone. During the one time in my career when I didn't feel like I had that person to interact with each day, I made my first foray onto Twitter and education blogs to find that connection online. Connecting with someone outside your setting can help you grow in different ways. It can help challenge what you know as a teacher, and help you see that there are other experiences that are possible in the world of schools.

Consider finding a PD pen pal. Find someone you can write a weekly (or monthly) letter to. There is a certain beauty and defined art in writing a handwritten letter, folding it so it will fit properly into the envelope, and placing a stamp so that you can later drop it into a mailbox to be sent a world away (or just across town) with your innermost thoughts about your successes and failures. While it is not the instant fix that social media provides, writing a letter, and the anticipation of receiving a handwritten letter back (when was the last time you received a handwritten letter in the mail?!), can help infuse some energy into your PD experience. Share your thoughts on a book that has helped you improve your practice. Write about a lesson that went really well—or was horrendously bad. Writing by hand can be cathartic and can provide a break from the instant excess of social media. Try it today!

Share a space: As a young teacher, I had the chance to work with an in-class support teacher for a full-day inclusion program. Cindy, who would become my first "partner in crime," moved her desk into our classroom, and we shared the space for a few years before she was assigned to a different set of students. During our time together, we had the chance to bounce ideas off each other and try different things while embracing the feedback we could provide to each other. In my role as an instructional coach, I had the chance to move into an office with someone hired as a technology integration coach. Even though we only spent one year in that shared space, it served as a period of tremendous growth for me, as Cindy challenged me to think differently and reexamine what I knew as an educator. That year alone propelled me to rethink what professional development could be.

What is so powerful about a shared space? It can force you to interact with someone who brings a different perspective than you do. You will hear different ideas. You will consider thoughts you hadn't considered before. You will spend time reflecting based on conversations with the person you are shar- ing the space with. You may need to compromise on certain activities and experiences by sharing a space. The time spent working with another person in such close quarters will ultimately help you grow as an educator. The opportunity to share a space may not come along very often, but if it does, embrace the chance to grow. Consider inviting a colleague who lacks a defined space to house their desk in your classroom. Make your intentions known to your administrator: that you would love to work in an inclusion setting or a coteaching scenario. Offer to work with a student teacher. Whatever opportunity presents itself to share a space with someone, take it the first chance you get!

Adopt a coconspirator. I was lucky. I met my coconspirator shortly after I was hired for my first teaching job. We didn't become coconspirators at that time, but we began to build the seeds of what would come later. Trevor Bryan and I quickly figured out that we held similar viewpoints about education although we came from different backgrounds and had different educational experiences. While Trevor was the art teacher and I was a fifth-grade teacher, he began to spend a lot of extra time in my classroom as we worked on several projects with students. We decided that there were many connections that could be made between math (one of my primary subject responsibilities) and art. We jokingly came up with the name "mARTh" when we would work on a shared project together.

All of our work together eventually led us to create the Four O'Clock Faculty website and blog, which has served as the springboard for much of what we share with the world. Even after I transitioned to a new district, we found a way to connect. Whether it was through weekly phone calls, text messages, or later Voxer, we found a way to continue challenging each other. Nearly twenty years have passed, and Trevor and I still find our partnership to be meaningful and valuable. Again, I was lucky to find my coconspirator quickly. Some people search for many years and don't find anyone who can fill that role.

My best advice is to find that person and stick with them. It's the person who will listen to your ideas. The person who will tell you when one of those ideas sounds like a disaster, and when maybe, just maybe, you have an idea that might turn into something. It's the person who will attend conferences with you and will share the drive and a meal while keeping the conversation going. You need a coconspirator to help you grow as an educator. If that person is not currently in your life, then maybe you need to expand your circle of friends. Find the person who will go ROGUE with you, the person who will challenge you to be a better educator, the person who will grow and learn with you, the person who will challenge you to be a ROGUE Leader.

Ask for Help!

Self-care can be big business. Health insurance companies and medical professionals realize that preventative measures can help people live healthier lives. In addition, the medical community realizes that healthier people lead to fewer medical operations and procedures and thereby minimize costs over the long term. Take advantage of the increased attention and focus on preventative health measures and ask for help!

In several of my previous roles, we have been able to partner with a number of groups to help increase self-care efforts for teachers. During a planned edcamp in my previous district, we partnered with a large local physical therapy and rehabilitation center to provide massage therapy for teachers. The organization sent three massage therapists out to our school, and we cleared space in the school library to set up massage chairs and tables. During the edcamp sessions, teachers had the choice to attend any session they wished or to sign up for a twenty-minute massage time in the library. By the end of the day, more than fifty teachers had taken advantage of the generosity of the rehabilitation group. All of this was free of charge to the district!

In a previous setting, I worked closely with our district's health and wellness committee to find ways to help our teachers practice self-care. In researching different options for teachers, we found that our district's health insurance company offered financial support for preventative self-care measures. The company provided the district with wearable fitness trackers for teachers. Friendly competitions were built into the school day. One teacher organized a walking group for students during recess. We purchased an additional thirty pedometers that students could use as they walked during recess. Our teacher leader had students record steps and created a map of how far students would have walked across the United States during the school year. It was an awesome way to recognize students for their efforts, practice a little geography, and promote self-care and a healthy lifestyle.

Self-Care Strategy: *Build in time for a walk!* I've seen grade-level partners walking during their lunch time. I've seen teachers and students walking together during their recess period. I've taken part in Podcasts and Pedometers sessions where teachers gather and listen and get their steps in for the day. However you can build in opportunities for students and colleagues to walk during the day, do it. Promote a daily walking club for fifteen minutes before or after school. Organize a walk-or-bike-to-school day once a week for those who are able to. Make your next staff meeting a walk-and-talk session. Whatever way you can, promote the power of walking!

Go Big And Do It All!

With some of the other strategies already presented in this chapter, you can start to build a culture of well-being at your school or within your district. If you begin with one of these ideas, you can start to make a dent. If you combine all of these ideas, you can create an event that firmly establishes well-being as a priority among colleagues.

Host a health and wellness fair for staff members that demonstrates a commitment to a healthy lifestyle. Think of an expo that combines the best of what is being done in the district, with outside organizations and groups that can help promote healthy living. Bringing back our massage therapists? More, if possible. This event is about going big! Inviting a local chef to teach healthy cooking habits or meal planning? Of course. Hosting a mindfulness session where teachers can learn techniques that work for them as well as students? Yes, yes, and yes.

Now, you might be saying to yourself, this sounds great, but it sounds like a lot of work, and a huge time commitment. It might be, and this is the important part. Going big means that you are going to need help. Find those ROGUE friends and form a health and wellness team. Some districts might require one. Even better, find those who are interested in promoting staff well-being. One of my go-to colleagues for a few years now has been a physical education teacher. He was interested in promoting a healthy lifestyle, and he got excited whenever I brought an idea that he could run with. (You might remember him from earlier in the chapter when he helped to organize Human Hungry Hungry Hippos! Thanks, Shaun!) School nurses often make a great addition to the health and wellness team, bringing a wealth of expertise and contacts that help in planning such an event. Finally, find those colleagues who bring expertise outside of the classroom: the teacher whose daily stretching and yoga routine is legendary among colleagues, the teacher who organized a morning running club for students, the custodian who has run multiple Ironman competitions, the food-services coordinator who is committed to healthy meal options for students and staff. There are many colleagues you may not know would be interested in this work and committed to pulling off a health and wellness fair. You just have to do some groundwork to find them!

After you have your team, decide on your priorities. What types of sessions and features do you want to present to staff at the wellness fair? You could have mini fitness stations located around the school. At the same time, staff members can check out a number of different sessions offered by experts. Bring in authorities on healthy eating, mindfulness, and exercise. Find a local restaurant to provide smoothies for staff. Create a relaxation room where staff can see what type of techniques can also be used with students. Your goal should be to help staff find ways that they can focus on their own well-being throughout their rituals and routines. You'll want staff to take whatever they learn at the wellness fair and carry it forward into their daily lives.

Once you have your plan in place, it's time to deliver! Make sure you ask each team member to take on different assignments. Many hands make for light work. Consider asking other colleagues who are not on the team to chip in. Ask for help outside of the school organization. Local businesses and community partners can lend their expertise, services, and resources. Pick a date that works for everyone. Consider a time during the school year when staff may be experiencing a lull. Where I'm located in the northeastern United States, the winter months begin to drag and wear on teachers by February and March. This is the perfect time to bring some excitement to the staff. Maybe you want to kick off the year with your wellness fair. You can bookend your year by kicking off with a big event, then follow up in May or June and share strategies and resources for staff to keep their wellness practices going over the summer. Remember, the goal is not a single event that is forgotten quickly, but rather memorable practices that continue to motivate staff and help them relieve stress and anxiety.

As educators, we might often associate self-care with being selfish. It's not. We can do things to focus on our own well-being that help us to be better educators. Focusing on our own health with mindfulness strategies and exercise not only makes us better educators but better people as well. As the quote says at the beginning of the chapter, we must be able to share our best with the world, not what's left. We can't drain ourselves so much that we have nothing left to give to everyone else.

Let's make sure that part of our professional learning is focused on not allowing our profession to continue to feel burned out. Yes, teacher burnout is a real thing, but so are powerful professional communities that are fighting it through dedication to teacher well-being.

ROGUE Leader Reflections

PD Keys

- Teacher burnout is real. Be sure to dedicate PD time to the physical, social, and emotional well-being of teachers.
- Sometimes teachers need a break from PD . . . and it can help their productivity and energy levels in the long run.
- Teaching can sometimes feel like working in a silo and managing the burden all by yourself. Give teachers the chance to connect with each other.

A Question to Ponder

How does your school focus on improving the physical, social, and emotional well-being of teachers?

PD Checkpoint #7: Collect $200 as You Pass Go!

During the summer when I was ten years old, I was sent to day camp. I remember free time in the afternoon on rainy days when we couldn't get outside to enjoy a great kickball game. Instead, we would play Monopoly games that would last a couple of hours until it was time to be picked up for the day. As a ten-year-old, you play Monopoly with a fierce ruthlessness. You do everything in your power to attain as much money and as many assets as you can. (I guess some adults still play the game this way!)

It would be nice to see a PD department in each school district that attains a small arsenal of money and assets. Professional development in most districts doesn't work this way, though. We don't usually see all of the district's assets and money going toward quality PD.

Let's imagine the opposite situation exists.

Pretend that you have Mr. Monopoly's unlimited supply of money and assets to deliver your next PD session.

What would the session look like?

_____

_____

_____

_____

_____

Who would be the presenter or facilitator?

_____

_____

_____

_____

What types of supplies or resources would you provide for participants?

_____

_____

_____

_____

_____

Knowing that you don't have an unlimited bank account to support your next PD session, how can you bring these ideas to fruition without the bankroll?

PD Rule #8: Time Is Precious. Don't Waste It.

A simple rule: Don't waste time. Don't waste your own time. Especially don't waste other people's time. And yet we've all sat through a professional development workshop where we felt like our time was wasted. We've experienced a blatant lack of respect demonstrated for the only thing that matters: our precious time. Why is that time wasted? In some cases, it might be a session that we are not interested in attending or we've been forced to join. Sometimes, it's a meeting that seems promising, but ends up crashing down around you minute by painful minute. Most of the time, it's the laundry list of other things that you could be doing that make you realize how wasteful someone else is being with our precious time.

So, what do we do about it? As Sam Levenson points out, "Don't watch the clock; do what it does. Keep going." Occupy your time with meaningful and relevant learning. If you attend a gathering that is not meeting your needs, excuse yourself and work on something that becomes a better use of your time. Find something more important.

I should probably provide a little clarification on Rule #8, as there is some important thinking that goes into it.

Rule #8: don't waste time.

8a: *don't waste your own time.*

8b, which is even more important: *don't waste someone else's time.*

8c: always *start and end on time*; refer back to 8b.

8d: *don't use more time than you actually need*; again, refer back to 8b.

This last sub-rule really needs to be examined in our professional development settings. You might actually find that you are truly engaged and learning during the first fifteen minutes of a session, but then bored and uninterested for the remaining forty-five minutes. Chances are this gathering should only have been fifteen minutes in the first place. You can learn a lot in a very short amount of time.

As a PD presenter, don't waste anyone's time.

As a PD attendee, don't let anyone else waste yours.

Chapter 8

Flexible Options for Busy/ Overwhelmed Educators

"You can do anything, but not everything."

—David Allen, *Getting Things Done: The Art of Stress-Free Productivity*

When I was in college, I would go to one of the three computer labs on campus and connect to the internet for my research, in addition to making my trips to the library for my "real" research using microfilm. At the same time, if I wanted to watch a particular TV show, I needed to be in front of my television at a specific date and time. The term "must-see TV" was coined at this time in the nineties and spoke to actually needing to be in front of the television when the show aired. If you missed it, you'd better hope that someone had recorded it to a VHS tape using their VCR. All of this seems so crazy now! Computer labs, microfilm, VHS tapes, VCRs, cassette tapes. My children would have no idea what any of these things are, but at one time, they were the height of technology.

Our world changed profoundly with the widespread adoption of the internet. When someone came along and put the full power of the internet into our pockets twenty-four seven, we were really on to something. No more computer labs. No more VCRs. No more microfilm. Practically anything that you could ever want or need can be found somewhere on the internet. Everything has gone digital.

And with this profound shift, learning has also changed deeply and forever.

So with this complete upending of the learning process, how did we adjust our professional development structures?

We didn't! We left them the same. We work in schools that have largely remained the same for the last one hundred years. Change is hard! It's difficult. It forces us to think differently. So we left our PD practices in place. It was easier that way!

Many of us work in schools which still have monthly faculty meetings after school where the whole staff gathers in the cafeteria and sits on hard benches to listen to the agenda be read for an hour. (If we are lucky, we get to do this twice a month!) It doesn't look much different from the way it did a decade ago, or two decades ago, or three decades ago or even four decades ago. Somehow, we are stuck in the sands of professional development time! Our professional development sessions shouldn't serve as a museum of all of our past practices.

Plus, there are far more efficient, easier, and better ways of doing things now. Back to those supercomputers sitting in our pockets at all times. Professional development no longer needs to be confined to a single time or place for every person, with every person in the room learning the same thing.

Professional development must provide flexibility for educators who are too busy, pulled in too many directions, and too overwhelmed. We are not trying to re-create "must-see PD" where everyone needs to be in the same room at the same time on the same topic. We need to shift our mindset and deliver PD that is on demand. This type of model can serve *all* our educators better, offering meaningful and relevant learning that is available when and where they see fit.

So how can we deliver flexible, on-demand learning for our colleagues? Try some of these activities to get started:

Digital Newsletters or Updates

One of the best and easiest ways to share information/new learning with colleagues is in a digital form. The ROGUE Guide highlighted the 1-5-15 Newsletter and the power of short reflection or learning activities. Each week, I share a brief Friday Focus with staff using Smore newsletters (www.smore.com). The formatting is super user-friendly, and once you come up with a format you like, you can duplicate the structure and change your basic information each week. In addition to logistics and schedule information for the upcoming week, I also share several links to online articles, blog posts, or videos that I think teachers may be interested in. I love when a colleague will find me on Monday morning and share that they will try something in their classroom based on something they saw in the Friday Focus.

I also love receiving these types of newsletters from colleagues. Our technology facilitators use Wakelet (www.wakelet.com) to share resources, new tech tools, and video tutorials each month. I can spend ten to twenty minutes on a Sunday evening learning about something I previously had no experience with. It's such a simple way to share and connect on ideas. No matter your role in education—teacher, administrator, coach, curriculum supervisor—a weekly or monthly digital newsletter can be a powerful learning tool.

Snow Day PD

It's a now-frequent educator ritual (at least here in my neck of the woods)! You hear about the impending storm. You check online to see the predicted snowfall amounts. Whatever the expected amount, you hope for more. On the way home from work, you stop at the grocery store to grab your bread, milk, and eggs. You stand in the incredibly long line like everyone else. You get home and wait for the early cancellation phone call. It is always nice to get the early call because then you can sleep in a little longer. When it doesn't come, you put on your PJs inside out and place your spoon in the freezer. (Good-luck charms, in case you are unfamiliar and need a snow day to happen!)

When the phone call comes way too early to let you know that school is closed for the day, you end up too excited to go back to sleep! And this serves as the perfect opportunity to learn something new. Options abound:

- You can pick up that latest professional development book you haven't had time to read.
- You can log onto Twitter and jump into #SnowDayPD to share your learning or to learn from others.
- You can connect online via Google Meet to start a relevant conversation about how to truly make learning more learner-centric.
- You can write a blog post to reflect on your own learning.
- You can explore a new learning experience for students that you wouldn't normally have time to check out.

Just like when you were a kid and a snow day gave you freedom to do whatever you wanted, a PD snow day can give you the freedom to learn in whatever way you want as an educator. Take advantage of the day!

CoffeeEDU

One of the most powerful professional development experiences happens once a month without much planning. Someone from your professional learning network sends out a message on Twitter, and suddenly twenty-five educators show up at a local coffee shop on a Sunday morning to learn from one another. (You can also search the hashtag #CoffeeEDU to find others who may be meeting in your area!) There is power to be found in the conversations that take place. Sometimes, it might be a discussion of a struggle and a minor suggestion that might help the person struggling. Sometimes, it might be a success shared with the group that sparks an idea for someone else. Sometimes, it might simply be commiseration and camaraderie. On occasion, new education books are raffled off as prizes or a book exchange takes place. I bring a book I've read that helped me and I pass it on hoping it will help someone else. I, in turn, leave with a book that will help me move forward. CoffeeEDU provides the true spark for professional sharing: passionate educators who show up not because they have to but because they want to. They want to learn. They want to share. They want to connect. They want to make education better.

Why Leave the House? Consider Other Virtual Options!

If we have learned anything, we know that at-home options have become the go-to for busy educators. People who are stuck at home or trying to squeeze in PD in between errands, responsibilities, and other tasks often take advantage of virtual options when they exist. We also have now experienced what professional development looks like when we aren't able to meet to learn together. During school shutdowns, we were forced to rethink PD on the fly. We had to figure out how to deliver quality professional development for teachers who needed professional learning quickly and remotely.

Distance learning. Remote learning. Online learning. Everyone scrambled to come up with something in order to help students learn at home. Educators are normally trained months to prepare for teaching an online class, and in this case, everyone was forced to throw together a plan within forty-eight hours. To steal a line from someone much smarter than me, it was the best of times and the worst of times.

And during all of it, as we struggled to take care of our own families and our school families, what we didn't realize we needed was the connection of professional learning! We were so worried about all that was happening around us and needed to count on something. So we naturally shifted toward the one thing that we have always needed in order to be great educators—professional connection!

It was really simple. Suddenly, it was harder to have those professional conversations with people we trusted to help us improve as educators. No more edcamps on Saturday afternoons. No more CoffeeEDU on Sunday morning. Hell, we couldn't even have a conversation in the faculty room with a colleague.

It was difficult, yes, so what did we do? Well, we are educators, so we improvised. We hunkered down in front of our computers and put in the hard work required to stay connected to our students and to each other. If it happens again for any reason, we will be better prepared. And we will have a number of options:

Virtual conferences: Many options popped up with most educators confined to their devices and homes. Many free online conferences provide great choices, while some paid options deliver powerful PD. You can easily find a conference that delivers exactly what you are looking for, and still wear your comfy pants. Win-win!

Virtual book clubs: Lots of educators picked up books and took advantage of extra time at home. It's simple. Find a few ROGUE friends and pick a book to spark your creative fire (*Creative Trespassing* by Tania Katan, *Creative Quest* by Questlove, or *Steal Like an Artist* by Austin Kleon) or pick up a book just for fun or get your mind off of everything, even if just for a few minutes.

#RemoteCoffeeEDU: Several times throughout the year, a group of passionate educators in my local area gather together on Sunday morning bright and early at 8 a.m. (sometimes 9 a.m. depending on who's organizing!) to chat and converse about education. It's great to see everyone, pick up a cup of coffee, and share in the powerful advice, strategies, and discussions that occur without a preset plan or agenda. If stranded at home, however, the conversations need to move online. During a #RemoteCoffeeEdu online, many jumped in to share their

thoughts on the new learning process associated with remote learning. Other educators used online face-to-face meeting tools like Zoom or Google Meet to share the connection and conversations in a virtual world. And every educator who participates in these types of conversations is better off for it.

Digital Appy Hour: Teachers learned more in a short time about what works online and what doesn't. We used new tools and resources, and it's important to share the tools that we found most successful. Find a group of willing learners, connect online, and share the latest tech tools, web resources, or helpful apps. Add everything to a Padlet for easy sharing! (Padlet is an online tool that allows you to organize and share information.) For more info about how one educator imple- mented a virtual Appy Hour, check out the Four O'Clock Faculty guest blog post "Virtual Appy Hour" by Starsha Canaday. (See QR code.)

PD Slackers: Slack has taken over the business world but has yet to find a stronghold in education. Use the Slack app to streamline com- munication and create a network of like-minded colleagues. Invite those who are helping to revolutionize PD, and share your best ideas via Slack channels. Use the tool to communicate and as a platform to host your best PD collaborations!

Voice PD: What can we share with a simple voice memo? If I've learned anything from the explosion of podcasts, it's that listening to someone can have an impact. Try incorporating voice PD into your weekly routine. Record an idea or brief PD message and share it with colleagues each week.

OMG PD (Online Mastermind Group): If you've ever worked with a Mastermind group, you understand the power of connection. The idea behind a Mastermind group is that two or more heads are better than one. Working with others to help solve problems that you are each dealing with can be a powerful tool for continuing your learning.

If you used to meet in person, now is the perfect time to take your Mastermind group online.

Device-free PD: Right now, there are not many PD opportunities that can happen without a device. While we are sometimes forced to connect via online platforms, we are reliant on the technology to help us bridge the social gathering divide. How can you disconnect instead? Device-free has only one rule. You guessed it. Any PD goes, as long as it's device free. Conversation with a colleague? Perfect! Reading a new book? Great! Writing a reflection and planning journal? Why not?

When in School, Do as the Learners Do . . .

Sometimes, you actually need the physical connection and motivation of talking with a colleague. Virtual learning can be great, but sometimes you just need to sit down and chat in order to pick someone's brain or just to find out about something new that they tried. Flexible, on-demand learning can include in person opportunities that offer a variety of chances during the week to learn in short periods of time.

Each day serves as the perfect opportunity to take on some new professional learning. Just five to ten minutes daily can serve as inspiration and motivation to continue your own learning. Try these quick learning and reflection activities to grow professionally:

Monday Morning Meeting: Gather your ROGUE friends to start the week and share something that you learned over the weekend. It could be a lesson from a book you read, or an idea that came to you during a trail walk. The Monday Morning Meeting gives you an opportunity to connect and share with colleagues who will challenge you to be better. If those ROGUE friends are not in your building, connect with them online or via phone. Start your week off right with some positive energy and inspiration. If you make this a regular habit, meaningful conversation and projects will come out of this meeting time.

Simple Protocol: Set a timer for fifteen minutes. Give everyone a chance to speak. No one can share a second time before everyone in the group has shared once.

Try It Tuesday: How will you take a risk and gamble on one of those ideas you came up with? Try out that new idea on Try It Tuesday! Find an adventurous colleague or two and discuss something you'd like to try with your students or in your classroom. Always wondered what it would be like if you read aloud to your high school students? Try it. Thinking about redesigning your classroom to improve workflow? Try it. Sharing your idea out loud can help transform it from half-baked concept to a strategy worth trying. Gather feedback and suggestions from your colleagues, and find time within your day to give it a go!

Simple protocol: Share out your idea with several colleagues. Each person must provide feedback on the idea. Once feedback is provided, refine the idea, and schedule a time to implement.

Walkabout Wednesday: Midweek serves as the perfect time to connect, collaborate, and share. Grab a colleague after school (preferably one who you don't connect with all that often). Take a walk for a few minutes with that colleague and discuss something that you are working on or struggling with. As you walk and talk, hopefully you and your colleague can generate solutions and strategies to help you both grow as educators.

Simple Protocol: Meet up in a centralized location in the building. Each week, choose a new partner. Walk for about five to ten minutes. Share in a meaningful way.

Thoughtful Thursday: Not quite the end of the week, but almost there. Thursday provides a great time for direct reflection. Meeting up with a reflection partner on Thursday mornings can help you to better take advantage of the last two days of the week. Talk with your colleague about what has gone well during the week, or what you'd like to fix. This contemplation session can help you and your students to focus your efforts on Thursday and Friday.

Simple Protocol: Meet with a reflection partner, someone you can share with, and who will provide honest feedback and support. Take turns answering three questions:

- What went well this week?
- What did not go well this week?
- What will my focus be for the remainder of the week?

Friday Afternoon Follow-up: Friday afternoons always served as one of my most important times as a teacher. After all my students were safely on their buses and most of my colleagues were already out of the building, I would sit quietly at my desk, reflecting on the week, catching up, and planning for the next week. While my weekly routine took me about an hour, it allowed me to clear my head for the upcoming weekend and allowed me to leave everything for Monday. There is a certain beauty that lies in the quiet of Friday afternoons. It always allowed for me to reach a peaceful state before I walked out the door.

Simple Protocol: Sit at your desk or work area. Follow through on any paperwork that needs to be finished. Reply to any pressing emails. Read that article or blog post that you tagged earlier in the week. Create a Monday to-do list so that you can let go of the pressures and worries of the week, and so you can enjoy the weekend!

As educators, we are busy folks. There's always a million things to do, and we can sometimes get bogged down in the logistics and minutiae of daily tasks. Time for PD is not something that is easily found. There's not a lot of extra time sitting out there just waiting to be used. As educators dedicated to our own growth and professional development though, we need to make time. We need to create opportunities that provide on demand learning for our busy lives. A podcast on the drive home. A lunch conversation with a colleague. Sunday morning CoffeeEDU. Ten minutes here. Twenty minutes there. It all adds up to make us better educators.

As the educator John Spencer says, "Stop wearing busy as a badge of honor." Use your time meaningfully, productively, and wisely. Stop counting minutes, and instead, make those minutes count.

ROGUE Leader Reflections

PD Keys

- Some of our PD structures have remained static for many years, but they don't have to continue this way. Shifting to on-demand PD can help to meet the needs of each and every educator.
- Virtual and remote learning opportunities now make it easy for teachers to learn anytime, anywhere. We no longer have any excuses.
- Daily professional learning sessions of just five to ten minutes can help educators to maintain professional connections while helping to provide inspiration and motivation to continue learning.

A Question to Ponder

How can we build PD opportunities into our daily routines and make it easier for educators to learn anytime, anywhere?

PD Checkpoint #8: PD All for One, and One for All?!

We have already discussed that one-size-fits-all (or most) PD is not the way to go. Another quote from Alexandre Dumas's novel *The Three Musketeers* actually requires more consideration when it comes to professional development: "Never fear quarrels, but seek hazardous adventures."

Now we are talking. PD as hazardous adventures! Think about how you can build some adventure into your professional development offerings.

How can you build "adventures" into your next PD session?

_____

_____

_____

_____

What type of "hazards," stumbling blocks, or obstacles can you build in to foster critical thought and reflections?

_____

_____

_____

_____

PD Rule #9: There's No Such Thing as Bad PD?

I'm sure most of you have heard of the saying "There's no such thing as bad pizza." I'm not quite sure if I can agree with this statement. There's been more than a few occasions when I've had a slice of bad pizza. It seems like it shouldn't be that hard when you are combining sauce, cheese, and dough, but alas, I've eaten more than a few slices that tasted like cardboard.

For rule #9 I'm going to attempt to apply the same principle. There's no such thing as bad PD. Again, it seems like it shouldn't be that difficult. Gather some educators. Pick a meaningful and relevant topic, and let educators learn from each other.

I know exactly what you are thinking: "But wait! In _The Four O'Clock Faculty_, you wrote an entire chapter about what to do if you faced bad PD." You got me. I did write about bad PD. Just like bad pizza, we know it still exists. So why the rule then?

I'm going to add a clarifier that's going to make all the difference.

Rule #9: there's no such thing as bad (self-initiated) PD.

That's right. If you are taking your PD into your own hands, then you will learn something. Gathering a few colleagues to discuss your grade level or department curriculum? Leading a group to explore new classroom technology resources? Leading a discussion at a staff meeting? All of these sound like productive uses of professional development time. Why? Because you are taking responsibility for your own learning. The PD will be significant and should have an impact on your students.

NOTE: all of the scenarios I wrote about previously still apply. If you take PD into your own hands and make the wrong choice of session, you need to follow through in order to get something out of it. Find a resource online. Get up and go do something more relevant. Research a new tech tool. The power *and* responsibility still lie with you.

Initiating your own PD means that you will learn no matter what. You know what you need. You know what's going to help. You know how you should be spending your time.

When you are taking charge over your own professional learning, there is no such thing as bad PD.

Chapter 9

Expertise

"Sometimes the greatest PD is the
teacher down the hall."

—Brian Aspinall

In high school, I took three years of Latin. While the other offerings of Spanish, French, and Italian might have been better choices, I thought Latin would give me a stronger background in vocabulary and help me when it came time for the SATs. After my three-year excursion, I did find myself more interested in the etymology of words. One of my favorite parts of watching the annual Scripps National Spelling Bee is when kids figure out a word based on its roots.

If you look up the etymology of the word "expert," you will find roots in Latin and French. You'll find words like "experienced," "practiced," and "skilled." You will see words like "tried" and "proven." The experts are those who are practicing in the classroom, tried and proven, who have developed particular skills in order to gain experience as strong educators.

We often go outside of our organizations to seek expertise for professional development purposes. We find the expert on trauma-informed instruction or social-emotional learning. The difficulty usually lies in the fact that a district may bring this person in for only one or two sessions with staff members. It's hard to maintain continuous learning with this type of model. Sometimes it's acceptable when the expert brings a highly developed skill set to the table. They might be able to deliver the kickoff to extended learning in a particular subject area.

What we often fail to remember, however, is that those in our own classrooms have been practicing and have often developed expertise that can help their colleagues. Those who are tried and proven and bring their experience to the table are those teachers who work with our students every day. Each one of us may bring a different area of expertise based on our background knowledge. We need to be able to rely on each other to grow as educators. Little did we know that the experts were right here all along. Start by finding those experts who are in direct proximity to you. Look for those local experts who can share their authority and experience to help everyone grow.

Find your local experts and share these strategies:

Workshop Wednesday

Susan Kotch posted a social media post about a practice from her school where someone who has expertise to share is given a sub for the day and then joins other teachers during their preps to teach them a new skill. It's a win-win, as staff learn something new from a colleague and that colleague is there to support everyone in learning the new skill. The admin team values the expertise staff members are bringing enough to have them share with colleagues.

Educational Experts
by Trevor Bryan

Often, professional development is geared toward helping everyone to learn everything equally.

But what if every teacher over the course of a year (or two) dedicated themselves to becoming an expert in one specific area?

Imagine having teachers who were experts in STEAM, or classroom management, or literary essays, or questioning, or teaching word problems, or sketchnoting, or creating clubs, or communicating with families, or reaching hard to reach students, or engagement, or mindfulness, or movement in the classroom, or alternative seating, or creating videos?

I'm not talking about going to one workshop or visiting one school. I'm talking about being valued and being encouraged and supported to do a deep dive into a topic of interest, exploring, researching, experimenting, questioning, and connecting, just like we ask our students to do.

What would happen if every teacher became an educational expert in one thing?

Connect with a Nearby College or University

Each semester, I go to one of our local universities and speak to undergraduates about my journey in education. By sharing my peaks and valleys, I hope to better prepare our future educators for the classroom. In turn, I also try to learn as much as I can from them. Our future educators are directly involved in the schooling process and can bring a different context and mindset to our schools. Invite the future educators into your building to support teachers. Most districts take advantage of local universities to bring on student teachers. The symbiotic relationship helps to give these students the necessary practice in becoming an educator, and the school can benefit in a number of ways, including inviting fresh ideas and invigorating passion into the building. I'm not sure that most schools utilize student teachers to the best of their abilities. Often, formal mentoring programs rely on those teachers who volunteer, but student teachers aren't carefully matched with mentors. It sometimes works out and sometimes doesn't. If you have a student teacher working in your building, get to know them. Have deep discussions about school and education. Pass on some of your expertise and find out where their expertise lies. Remember, we can always learn from everyone, not just those who have been in schools for many years. Plus, if you are a building administrator, it also helps during the hiring process to have an already established relationship with many of the job candidates.

Find the Parents Who Are Educators

Education is an incredibly small world. Eventually, you know someone who knows someone who knows someone, and somehow you are connected with an educator from across the country or world. But you probably also have parents of students in your own school who are also educators. They usually have a lot to share and, especially if they work in a different district, can provide a varied perspective. Use their expertise. Talk to them about what's working particularly well in their school or district. Find out how you can partner up to improve student learning outcomes in both districts. I gained a little extra enjoyment out of my daughter's field trips because I often had the chance while on the bus (and other downtimes throughout the day) to sit and chat with her teachers. I would often pick their brains to find out what types of projects and new initiatives they used to engage students. I hope that the conversations were equally beneficial for them.

Try the Silent Classroom Walk

There is so much to be learned from the colleagues that you connect with (or don't connect with) each day. You can even learn a great deal by simply taking a peek in their classrooms. What do you see? What do you notice? What does the classroom say about your colleague? Or your colleague's students? Set up a silent classroom walk, in which you and your colleagues visit each other's classrooms. Observe first. Give each person a stack of sticky notes and a pen. Write down your observations. After a fifteen- or twenty-minute period of visiting classrooms, come together to share and reflect. Share the sticky notes. Group similar observations. Have each person share one thing they took away from another classroom that they'll use to change their own classroom. Again, learn from your local experts.

Get to Know Community Experts

There is much to be learned from the experts in our communities who take the 20,000-foot view from outside education. Technology experts. Business leaders. Artists. Writers. Connecting to our community experts and, more importantly, their ideas can help us improve as educators. My Four O'Clock Faculty cofounder, Trevor Bryan, has been an art teacher for many years. Besides staying connected with the local artists in his community, he has partnered with the Princeton University Art Museum to improve his own practice (as both artist and educator). In addition, he works with parents and children at the museum on family days and even takes his own students on a field trip to the museum each year to practice comprehension and art appreciation skills as part of his Art of Comprehension program. The partnership allows him to provide an added opportunity for students to visit a world-class museum to experience art firsthand. Museum curators can lend their knowledge and experience to students to help them better understand art.

Welcome to the Committee on Committees!

Dear Committee Member:

Thank you for agreeing to serve on the Committee on Committees. While you were voluntold to participate, we thank you for agreeing and appreciate your participation.

Our first meeting will be next Wednesday from 9 a.m. to 3 p.m. We will take a sixty-minute lunch and several twenty-minute restroom breaks throughout the day. In order to make sure that we are prepared to get through the three-page agenda, our pre-meeting for the first meeting will be held on Tuesday from 12 to 3 p.m. The follow-up meeting will be on Friday from 11 a.m. to 3 p.m. in case we don't get through the entire agenda. (If we do manage to get through the agenda, we will use this time to recap what was discussed, along with some more breaks.)

Please be sure to review all of the relevant and related documents we have attached to this email. The attachments have been saved as Word documents. If you have any additions or changes, please save them on your computer and email them as attachments to the rest of the group. At a later date, we will meet to compile any changes or additions that exist within the dozens of emailed versions housed on each person's individual computer.

The purpose of this committee is to review our other committees to see if we can make our committee processes more efficient or to streamline any work flows. When reviewing inefficiencies, we will utilize our six-month review process to make any changes to policy, followed by a policy review period, and any final changes will be made within eighteen months. New policies and processes will then go into effect at the beginning of the following year.

The work that this committee will do is important. We may even consider some of the suggestions proposed by this committee for future changes. Once documented, all of the committee's findings will be housed online in a final document, which will also be printed as a hard copy, to be housed in the Committee on Committees binder at our district offices.

Again thank you for "volunteering" for our committee. We look forward to seeing you next week!

Sincerely,

Your committee leaders

Raise your hand if you've been asked to serve on a school-based or district-based committee before. OK, most of you are raising your hands right now.

Now, keep your hand raised if you chose to serve on that committee because you thought that the work would have a great impact on learning outcomes for students. Most of you still have your hands raised.

Finally, keep your hand up if you felt disappointed after your experience on that committee. Hmmmm . . . most hands are still raised.

Committee work in many schools and districts has the potential to help move our schools forward, but in practice it always fails to live up to the hype. Why? Part of it is meeting culture. Often committees delve into the territory of meetings for meetings sake. Action in many districts means the appearance of action. When a school or district commits to change but isn't necessarily ready for the actual change that would come from action steps, it can project the appearance of change via committee work. "We are absolutely committed to change! We formed a committee to explore our options." What usually arises from this type of strategy is a plethora of exploration and conversations, and a complete lack of actual actions to change things. "We formed a committee!" is the rallying cry of those interested only in the surface-level appearance of change and moving forward. The committee provides an opportunity to hide behind a process instead of actually making change.

So, how can you actually create committee work that turns out meaningful outcomes? Implement these changes to committee work to make it more productive and conducive to consequential actions.

Keep Committees Small

In my experience, committees always have to be created with representation from every corner of the school or district. This often leads to bloated teams that hinder actionable steps to be taken. I work with a team of twenty-three principals. Get us in the room and ask us to order pizza for lunch, and you will see a ninety-minute discussion about how many pizzas to order and what type of toppings should be featured. When the decision is finally made, many will ultimately be unhappy with the choices as they won't feel their thoughts and opinions were represented. When considering who to invite to a committee, the phrase "the more the merrier" is often used to provide a completely inclusive casting call. I have found, though, that the more people that are added, the more the decisions become difficult to make.

Invite enough people to include a variety of differing perspectives, but keep your committee small enough to allow for swift decision making. For example, if you are looking to form a committee at the building level that impacts K–5 math instruction, you might be well served by including one upper-grade-level teacher (grades three through five), one lower-grade teacher (grades K through two), and the basic skills teacher who serves all grade levels. For a differing perspective, you might also include a special education teacher as well. A committee made up of only three or four differing viewpoints will be able to explore the issue and important contexts and come to a decision without involving too many arguments that eventually lead to gridlock or non-decisions. While we don't want decisions by a committee of one, we also don't want non-decisions by a committee of twenty-five people.

Make Sure Committee Work Is Necessary and Voluntary!

In all my years of education, I have seen very few committees that were actually engaged in meaningful work. Again, a lot of the committees we form are intended to give the perception of action. It makes us feel good to say that we are doing something about issue X; we have a committee. Create a committee only when it is absolutely necessary. Standing committees that meet several times a year, regardless of whether there is any meaningful work to be done, simply waste everyone's time and energy. Create a committee only when you are looking for meaningful action.

This goes hand in hand with taking volunteers who want to take part in purposeful work. Too many times, we cajole, plead, and beg to convince people to participate in committee work. It's the reason the word "voluntold" exists. We ask for volunteers, feel bad about telling anyone no, and create standing committees that include dozens of volunteers. We make sure that there is at least one representative from each building, and administrators are left in the position of finding a "volunteer" to represent their building. Part of this problem can be eliminated by creating committee work only when needed. If we have fewer committees, we need fewer volunteers. With the need for fewer volunteers, we can recruit those who are truly interested in participating in order to take necessary actions.

Set Reasonable Time Limits

Long-winded three-hour marathon committee meetings don't serve much purpose. They can easily zap everyone's energy and take away from the true reason that the committee exists in the first place. Setting up multiple meetings also helps provide a buffer zone for committee work. When someone knows that a decision can be put off until the next meeting, it is much easier to put off making that decision. If I had a dime for every time I heard a committee member say, "Let's wait until next meeting to decide . . . " Committees should operate in a succinct and efficient manner, quickly reviewing necessary information and calling on members to make informed decisions to move forward.

Some general rules of thumb for committee work:

No committee meetings should go over an hour. Forty-five minutes is probably the sweet spot, but definitely don't go beyond sixty minutes. If it's your opening meeting, think ten minutes for introductions, twenty minutes to review pertinent information and share thoughts and opinions, twenty minutes to problem solve and create action steps, and ten more minutes for recap.

Eliminate any unnecessary follow-up meetings. Once you come out of your first meeting with action steps, it is really not imperative to meet again until you have followed through on the action steps. (For any necessary follow-up meetings, you can probably eliminate the portions involving introductions and fact-finding.)

Don't put off decisions. You might typically hem and haw about making decisions because sometimes you don't want to make a decision that will have an impact on others. You might seek more time to become "more informed," to have "all" the information before deciding on a course of action. I'm here to tell you that you will never have all of the information, and stall tactics don't make the decision process any easier. Decide when you can, and put actions into place. If the action steps work out, then great. If they don't, you go back to the drawing board and try again.

Action Steps Are the Name of the Game!

For any committee that you form or are involved in, you should outline three to five action steps of items that you want to accomplish through the work of the committee. Outline these action steps in your first meeting with your committee. Going back to the elementary math example presented earlier, briefly discuss what math instruction looks like in your building, discuss what it might look like under different circumstances, think about what resources teachers would need in order to begin to shift math instruction, and then create your list of action steps to get there. You might come up with three steps that you want to accomplish:

1. Provide more classroom infused math instructional coaching PD for teachers.
2. Provide more resources for teachers to include problem-solving, number sense, and critical thinking into the curriculum.
3. Provide specific resources to help teachers differentiate for a diverse group of learner needs.

While committee members can still update the committee on the status of these three action steps or work collaboratively to accomplish them, any additional committee meetings can wait until these action steps are completed. Once these things are in place for a period of time, you can then meet to discuss how the actions have impacted math instruction and student learning outcomes. Of course, during the process, you may need to make adjustments as necessary, but it all starts with concrete actions that you are willing to take to create a change.

Deliver on Action Steps

This is often where many committees get hung up, and they either continue meeting to keep revising the action steps or never meet again because they can't deliver on overly ambitious action steps. The actions chosen must be accomplishable. In the example provided previously, the three action steps might need to be broken up so that all committee members can actively work to put the actions into practice. Putting PD coaching sessions in place and creating resources for teachers are steps that will take some time to accomplish, but they are well worth the effort. As part of the committee, you need to make sure that the action steps don't simply become talking points about things that you "want" to accomplish, but rather things that are actually done to improve student learning outcomes. Remember, everything that we do in the name of professional development, even committee work, should have the lone goal of supporting students in the classroom.

The experts you need are all right there. They are in your building. They are in the building next door or across town. They might be at the local college or somewhere in your local community. The experts that you have needed all along are within reach. You just have to find them and connect with them. They are probably the people the district relies on to complete committee work—although the district processes may tie them up in committee work instead of encouraging them to take action. Find the experts. I am sure they will be willing to help. If you are an expert, take action into your own hands and begin to share your expertise. As Brian Aspinall points out in the chapter's opening quote, sometimes the best PD is the teacher down the hall. Take advantage of those local experts and learn everything that you can from them. Help them be better by sharing, and make yourself better by learning from them.

ROGUE Leader Reflections

PD Keys

- ⊶ PD experts are all around us. It's those who are tried and proven, experienced, and practicing their skills in the classrooms around us.

- Experts can also be found in the community. Let's connect our colleagues (and students!) with those outside education who can lend their knowledge, experience, and expertise.
- Committee work in our districts can often lend itself to surface level cosmetic fixes. Dig deep to allow for committees to take action steps to produce more efficient and meaningful work.

A Question to Ponder

How will you connect with experts in your school and community to become a better educator?

PD Checkpoint #9: The Name is Development, Professional Development

Your mission, should you choose to accept it, is to teach a colleague about a new resource, strategy, or tool.

Sounds simple. However, you need to remain incognito. Your colleague can't realize that you are teaching them something new.

Spend just ten minutes with them completing your mission.

Don't blow your cover.

Write about what you learned by teaching a colleague something new.

PD Session Planning: How to Reach the End of Your PD

Not a goodbye . . .

Not a see you later . . .

But instead, how did I grow?

Ending a PD gathering the right way can be the most challenging part. I've facilitated and hosted many sessions where I simply ran out of time. I'm embarrassed to admit the number of times I've had to say, "Sorry folks, we ran out of time. Here is my contact info if you have any questions." It's an awful way to send participants off. They rush out of the room hurried and frantic. You probably didn't share the meaningful words you planned on ending with, and you wasted another valuable opportunity to provide an impact on the professional growth of colleagues.

If you've run a successful PD session, teachers will leave having grown, and ready to take their learning back to their students.

It's all about the ending.

Before teachers leave your session, there is a technique you can use to send them off on the right foot and continue to build a stronger community of learners. It is an activity I have used with colleagues to close our staff meetings, and every time we use it, it helps to establish a powerful connection amongst our staff. It takes just a few minutes, and allows teachers to reflect on their learning, share gratitude, or repair a relationship with a colleague.

I first found the activity, called Appreciation, Apology, Aha! (AAA), on the Edutopia website. (See QR code.)

The video shows the activity as used with a group of students, but it also works really well for building community with colleagues.

No matter what type of PD activity you've just completed with colleagues, try to close out with AAA. Even if you've just finished a standard, traditional, boring, agenda-focused faculty meeting, you can send colleagues off in the right frame of mind. Save five to seven minutes at the end of your session and have participants stand in a circle around the perimeter of the room. The rules are simple. Each person gets a chance to share briefly. If they don't wish to share, they can simply say "Pass" and move on to the next person. They can share:

An *appreciation:* a concise thank-you or expression of gratitude to someone or something. It might be a simple nod to a grade level partner ("Thanks for all of your help this week with lesson planning") or a general expression of gratitude ("I'm really thankful that the weather cooperated with us this week"). We don't get to say "thank you" nearly enough. This provides another opportunity to do so.

An *apology:* Sometimes, we need to publicly express a regret or repair a relationship. Anyone sharing can contribute to the community by expressing their remorse for their impactful behaviors. I've occasionally kicked off our AAA with an apology at a staff meeting ("I'm sorry I haven't been as present and visible as I should have been over the past couple of weeks"). Teachers have apologized to colleagues for being frustrated or curt. The apology usually goes a very long way in building a strong community because it allows people to take responsibility for their actions and to try to repair the harm they've done. Colleagues usually appreciate the honesty and sincerity, and it can help to move everyone forward.

An *aha:* as responsible professionals, we should always focus on our own learning. Sharing an aha gives each person the chance to reflect or share something that they have learned. It might be something that they learned during the PD session ("I figured out a great way to use Google Sites to facilitate student blogging") or something that they learned in the classroom ("We tried 360-degree math this week and had excellent results"). Sometimes, one person's aha moment will spark another in thinking about a new concept or activity, and a natural collaboration is born. Sharing our learning helps to build and connect our community as well!

> **NOTE:** If you are hosting or facilitating a PD session and most attendees are strangers to you, you can opt out of the first two options here and simply share an aha moment at the end of the session. Continue to circle up and give anyone who wants a chance to share what they learned during the session. It will help everyone to consolidate their learning, and remind some people of the key takeaways from the session.

By implementing this simple activity at the end of a PD session or event, you can give participants a tangible result, a meaningful impact that they can carry back to their students and classroom. You will notice that colleagues will become more accountable for their actions and their own learning. They will learn and grow *together*, and it will all be visible!

After all, it's all about the ending, isn't it?

PD Rule #10: When in Doubt, If a Rule Is Not Working, You Might Have Only One Option. If You Must, Break the Rules.

Rules might typically stifle some. Struggling to shift the PD paradigm in your school because of stodgy contract rules, mandated PD content, and leadership playing it overly cautious? Well, you know what they say about rules . . .

I tried to come up with a solution for a logistical problem. We were trying to host a district-wide book study, but each of our buildings ended at a different time in the afternoon. We didn't normally have district-wide PD after school, because the teachers who finished earliest did not want to wait for the later schools to finish. So district-wide PD never happened after school. It wasn't so much a rule as it was a mandate by circumstance.

When I even suggested that we wait until 4 p.m. (when all schools were finished!) to host a meeting, my idea was quickly dismissed. "No way! I'm not going to sit around for an hour and a half while I wait for the other schools to finish."

Not one to be bound by any type of constraints, my mind went into overdrive to conceive a solution. "What if you didn't have to wait around?" I said, proposing another solution. "What if we just did it using Twitter at a time that worked for everyone?"

Some liked the idea. Some resisted. Some quickly suggested several rules that would not allow us to move forward with the idea. The contract would not allow for an additional meeting outside of the monthly building meeting and monthly curriculum meeting. We wouldn't be able to monitor participation to award PD credit hours. Teachers shouldn't be expected to log on to district-related work beyond their contractual hours. As usual, each of these barriers seemed like small hurdles to me. None of them seemed like a good reason *not* to move forward with the Twitter book study.

So in the end, we moved forward with the book study at 8 p.m. on Monday evenings with a big capitalized "VOLUNTARY" in front of the description.

As the popular online mantra goes, "Learn the rules like a pro, so that you can break them like an artist!"

And about forty teachers joined in each week to discuss and share their thoughts on the book we were reading. It worked despite all of the consternation about what could go wrong. Instead, we focused on what could go right.

In the end, rules are only there to bind you to a certain extent. They are often created because of a thing that happened once or in trying to avoid one specific problem from popping up.

And, I think that you may know this already, but sometimes, you just need to go ROGUE!

So, rule #10: break the rules if you must. Or better yet, make your own rules!

Make professional development better. Give it an edge that rivals some of the best PD you've seen. Improve it despite the limitations you are faced with. Don't accept no for an answer.

Do what you want. Do what you can. Improve PD no matter what. You have my permission to make your own rules or to break the rules if you must.

Chapter 10

Design Your Own PD

"The credit belongs to the man who is actually in the arena, whose face is marred by dust and sweat and blood; who strives valiantly; who errs, who comes short again and again, because there is no effort without error and shortcoming; but who does actually strive to do the deeds."

—Theodore Roosevelt

I have been working toward perfecting professional development for several years. And before you go and say, "You see, Rich, nothing could ever be perfect," you should know that deep down, I know and understand this, but I've also seen the possibilities. I have seen perfect moments related to PD. I've seen teachers engaged, sharing, collaborating, discussing, and finding joy in continuing their own learning. And I've seen how these educators then go back and have an impact on their students.

I've also seen those disaffected. It's always readily apparent when teachers would rather be anywhere else in the world than in the room for PD. Sitting waiting for their car to get an oil change, visiting their favorite local dentist, haggling with a salesperson over a used car, or maybe sitting through a seven-hour spoken word performance of the dictionary.

This is the hideous, horrible, and hidden heartache associated with professional development. There are moments when it can be perfect but also many more moments when it is quite less than perfect. In fact, those moments can be a complete and utter waste of everyone's time—the planner, the presenter, the attendees, and, most importantly, the students.

Many questions arise:

- How do we turn those moments into the movement?
- How do we ensure that professional development continues to grow in order to benefit educators and students?
- How do we create professional development opportunities that are continuous and ongoing?
- How do we convince all educators that they should be overturning the current professional development system to ensure that the PD sessions offered are meeting their needs (and their students' needs)?

Time for the big reveal. (In case you haven't figured it out yet!)

It starts with you.

That's right. The ROGUE PD movement begins and ends with you. Now that you've read this book (and maybe *The Four O'Clock Faculty*), you have plenty of ideas to try out. You've got plenty of background knowledge and information to begin to shift the PD paradigm in your setting. You've probably identified those who will assist in making PD amazing.

You are fully equipped to become a ROGUE Leader.

Of course, you may have your doubts. You are, after all, only one educator. You may be worried that you are not an administrator and therefore don't have the power to create change. You might be worried that you won't be able to convince others. You may be suffering from impostor syndrome, someone afraid that despite their knowledge they can't help others to grow. You are thinking to yourself: How much change can one educator create?

I'll say it again. You are fully equipped to become the ROGUE Leader that you were meant to be.

If you are still unconvinced, know that you, yes you, have the ability to shift professional development for yourself and others. You can be the ROGUE Leader that others desperately want and need. Others are seeking your guidance. It doesn't matter what title appears before or after your name. Your colleagues need you.

All it takes is one person to begin. One person can start to change everything. One person can begin the movement. One ROGUE Leader can set in motion the seismic shift that begins to make professional development better for everyone around them. And that one person is you.

It typically starts from the bottom. It's not usually a top-down approach because it requires the dedication and effort of those involved. As Teddy Roosevelt said, it starts with the person in the arena. It needs to begin with those who are in the thick of it—the teachers and educators who are in the trenches, doing the work every day. It also usually begins with something small. It doesn't have to be a major event, or a grand gesture to have an impact. It can start with a small action: asking a colleague to chat about something that works with their students, or sharing an article that you think will help your grade-level partner.

The movement usually starts small. It's like eating an elephant. One bite at a time.

What will you do now that you've read the book? How will you become a ROGUE Leader? What small steps will you take to begin to shift the PD dynamic in your setting?

You can begin with some simple action steps. Consider riffing on some of the ideas already shared in the book. How could you modify or improve on any of these ideas? Remix. Recreate. Redo. Add your own spin. Create PD that uniquely serves you. Begin with these activities for starters:

Attend a CoffeeEDU or edcamp event. Find an open Saturday or Sunday and connect with other passionate educators. While edcamps require more of a time commitment, usually clocking in at a few hours, a CoffeeEDU event only lasts one hour. Both will help to reenergize your spirit and to serve as a platform for better PD! Find those who are seeking to get better at their craft and begin to congregate with them. You will find that the conversations help you to grow and improve.

Can't find one locally? Start your own. Even though there are multiple edcamp and CoffeeEDU events across the country and world each weekend, you may find yourself in an area that doesn't support this type of learning. That's OK. You simply need to start your own. Find your ROGUE friends and get organized. Check in with your local coffee shop, and make sure they are good with a small crowd. (Spoiler alert: they are! They want customers.) Next, advertise your gathering and its date and time. Final step: show up and learn. Add some excitement by asking each participant to bring a favorite book for a book swap, or reach out to an educational publisher and request some books as giveaways. They will usually provide a few copies as door prizes! The other option is joining in online. With the increase in the number of online professional development opportunities, you may be able to join an online edcamp or virtual CoffeeEDU group if there is not one in your area.

Share some of your knowledge at your next faculty meeting. Administrators are just waiting for someone to come to them and offer to plan PD for the next staff meeting. Having been the one who designs the monthly staff meeting, and knowing that I try to incorporate as much PD as possible can be exhausting. I've loved the opportunities to collaborate with colleagues and switch up staff meetings when possible. Usually, it's a teacher who simply has something interesting to share. It can be a gentle nudge. *"I loved that writing lesson you did yesterday. Would you consider sharing that with staff at our next meeting?"* It could be unsolicited. If you have something that you think others would benefit from, offer up your services. Go to whoever plans your monthly staff meetings, and offer to present. If you are told no, keep at it. Be persistent. (Again, most administrators would welcome the help from a knowledgeable colleague!)

Organize others to share their expertise at your next faculty meeting. If you don't have something worthy of being shared at your next staff meeting, find someone who does. Talk to a colleague who does something amazing with their students. Ask them to present it at your next meeting. Find three or four teachers with amazing ideas and ask them to come together to help their colleagues learn. We are all experts in something. Find the experts and bring them together in the name of collaboration.

Host a lunch and learn. What could be easier? You are already halfway there if you plan on eating lunch today. Invite a colleague to join you as you eat lunch and listen to a podcast, or read an educational blog. Ask questions and share in meaningful conversation. Invite multiple colleagues, and present a new tech tool or instructional strategy. I've found that it's better to eat lunch with a small group in the classroom. (Sometimes, the faculty room and its distinct vibes just call for complaints and less than productive discussion!) Eat and plan your next unit. Better yet, plan a lunch and learn with students and have them teach you and colleagues the latest tech tools. It can be a win-win for everybody involved.

Start a Podcasts and Pedometers group. The beauty of listening to a podcast is that you can often multitask. You can listen as you participate in another activity. Find your cast of willing collaborators and organize a Podcasts and Pedometers group. Set a time to gather and walk each week as you listen to an episode. Have everyone listen to the same episode and discuss or let everyone choose their own podcast and share their learning. Get those steps in. Help those around you become healthier, fitter, and smarter.

Create a PD newsletter. Organize a combination of your best ideas, worthwhile resources, and teaching tips and dole them out to your coworkers. Use a user-friendly tech tool like Smore or Wakelet to organize the resources or simply send an email with links to the resources.

Find the simplest way to share with your colleagues but also ensure a friendly format that your ROGUE friends will gravitate toward. Also, be sure to be consistent. Share each week, and don't miss a week. While colleagues may not take away something each week, the consistent practice of sharing will ensure that teachers can find something when they need it.

Professional learning is the glue that holds the field of education together. None of us are better without strong professional development programs. It's up to all of us to improve professional development. It's also up to us to build something meaningful out of the PD opportunities that we are given.

Every one of us has a professional responsibility to be a ROGUE Leader. Each time that we sit through bad PD without providing feedback, without creating something meaningful on our own, without changing the PD paradigm, we are setting our profession back. Each of us has a responsibility to improve PD. It is on all of us to make it relevant, to make it work for our needs, to make it work for each other, and to make a difference for our students. Not only do each of us have a responsibility to ourselves to make it meaningful but we must hold each other accountable to ensure that professional development meets a certain quality threshold.

Often, the existing problem is that PD is something that is done *to* educators, not something that is done *with* educators. You might hear the line from an overwhelmed administrator who says "We gave the teachers PD on [insert any number of topics—student-centered instruction, the workshop model, block scheduling, and so on]. I'm not sure why they aren't doing it." In these types of situations, professional development is treated as something that is given to teachers to somehow bestow wisdom upon them. It's kind of like the star-on and star-off machines in Dr. Seuss's *The Sneetches*. The teacher enters the PD machine without knowledge of the topic and walks out ready to implement after one PD session. Teaching doesn't quite work that way. Professional development definitely doesn't work that way.

Professional development work (yes, it is work!) requires an engaged population. It takes an individual (or group) who is committed to the work of making PD better. It is the ROGUE Leader who is ready to make professional development a priority, someone willing to take the necessary small steps to create a big shift in professional development practice. Once you've mastered those small steps and created something purposeful, you can begin to build upon your success.

After you've started to build something meaningful, it's time to design your own PD! It's time to create with your intended audience in mind. For years, you've heard all of the complaints.

Not enough . . .

Too much . . .

It could have used some . . .

I could have done without . . .

Each of us serves as an expert on PD. Simply because it needs to be personally relevant to each of us.

If you are planning on becoming the ROGUE Leader I know you can be, you need to design PD that works for you and your colleagues. You need to create opportunities that work to engage educators as everyday learners.

Answer these simple questions and design your own PD that meets the needs of an engaged population:

Will the time spent be worthwhile? After you finish with your own designed PD, you must ask whether people will consider the time well spent. Will participants, including yourself, find that the professional development time was used wisely and productively? If everyone walks away having learned something, then the answer is a resounding YES!

Is this relevant to what I do each day? Often, the professional development we are forced to attend doesn't apply to our daily roles. Based on the title, it might sound like it loosely applies, but in fact, the PD session doesn't hold any relevance to our content area or specific job responsibilities. Every session must offer a connection to what we do, and give us the ability to apply what we learn to our work with students.

Will this make me a better educator? If I had a dime for every time I left a PD session thinking that it's had no impact on me as an educator. The ultimate goal of quality professional development should be to lift our profession, and each individual attendee. It should make each participant a better teacher and, more importantly, push them to want to continue learning more. Better can be a difficult term to define here, but even incremental improvement can help educators to further develop their practice.

Will this help my students? I've said it before, and I'll say it again and again. The goal of each PD session should be to help educators help students. Anything that a teacher ultimately learns should help to improve student learning outcomes. Not only do we want teachers to improve based on the professional development that they take part in, but we want that growth and learning to carry over to students. Good PD ultimately leads to improved practice and pedagogy for students.

How can I make this fun? Professional development can be downright boring, but it doesn't have to be. When PD is fun, teachers can be more engaged in the process. Figure out a way to make it enjoyable for educators. There could be a theme or hook that catches people's attention. It could be an active session in which engaging participation drives learning. Whatever way you can find to bring in some good old fashioned fun, do it. Any aspect of entertainment, amusement, or excitement will only help to engage participants more.

Am I interested in learning about this topic? If you have no interest in a PD topic, it does not matter how engaging, compelling, or thought-provoking the session is. Sometimes, I've been lucky and a session has slightly appealed to me based on the title alone. Even a little interest combined with a stellar session can go a long way. But if you have zero interest in a topic, it won't matter how great a session is. You'll struggle to get through the affair without thinking of a bunch of other things you could be doing. Design your own professional development around topics that you and your colleagues are interested in. Think of the topics that are discussed on a regular basis and start there!

Can I find others who will learn alongside me about this topic? This is where some of the other questions you've already answered will help when designing a PD session. If you've created something fun and interesting, you should be able to round up some colleagues who will be ready to join you in learning. This is the opportunity to involve your ROGUE friends—the individuals ready to take on any and all PD topics. Find others who will find joy in learning alongside you. It might be a colleague who challenges your thinking by asking just the right question at exactly the right moment, or someone willing to take their learning and implement it in the classroom along with you. Whoever you can find, you'll always learn more and have more fun when others are involved.

Is this meaningful? This is one of the most important questions you can ask yourself any time you are designing and planning your own PD. Professional development must be meaningful. It needs to have a substantial impact on you and your students. Every time. When designing a PD opportunity, you will need to determine the essential purpose. You should think about what you are trying to get out of the session. Do you want to discuss something? Plan something? Create something? Whatever your goal, you need to make sure that it is useful and important to the work that you and your students do.

Can I take this back to the classroom immediately? We've explored the idea that effective PD must have an impact in the classroom with students. If we develop the profession as we are supposed to, we need to see improvement in the classroom where it matters. Are students better served? Is the learning taking place able to change instruction immediately? Think about whether the session you are planning will be applicable in the classroom. Can educators take the ideas and content and implement them instantly? Is there a large learning curve for what you are presenting or discussing? Any time a teacher can leave a session with ready-to-go ideas, lessons, and tools, they are more likely to actually carry out those plans in the classroom.

You now have everything that you need.

- You've learned several PD rules that can help you as you continue your PD journey.
- You now understand why professional development is sometimes a dirty word in education.
- More importantly, you now know what you can do to change that perception.
- You have the READI framework as a guide to help you plan meaningful professional development programs and sessions.
- You understand why you need to bring your passion and find others that share your passion.
- You have some tools and strategies to reach those who may not share your full passion for PD.
- You've learned some tips for switching up staff meetings and beginning to change the status of the dreaded district PD day.
- You've learned how to engage participants during the beginning, middle, and end of PD sessions.
- Finally, you now know how to involve the experts around you to make PD better for everyone.

You are ready. You have all of the tools and resources to make better professional development a priority.

You also now have an invitation to do so. And permission.

I formally invite you to go out and change your own PD paradigm. If you've been waiting for the invitation, here it is.

Join the Revolution.
Become a ROGUE Leader!

Here is your invitation to change your own professional development paradigm!

- **Who:** Shift PD for yourself and others like you!
- **What:** Find or create meaningful and relevant PD that meets your needs.
- **Where:** In your school or district or with colleagues outside of your school or district.
- **When:** Right now. There is no better time! Don't wait.
- **Why:** If you don't take your own PD seriously, no one else will.
- **How:** You now have all of the tools and resources. Start with small steps that lead to big changes!

I also give you permission to go out and begin to shift your PD worldview. If you have come to realize that no one else is going to give it to you, and you've been waiting for it, then I grant you full permission to create meaningful PD. I fully authorize you to do what is necessary to improve your own professional learning.

Now that you are ready, willing, and able to support the cause, I hope that you will dig deep into your role as a ROGUE Leader.

As a ROGUE Leader, you can make the rules.

As a ROGUE Leader, you can inspire others.

As a ROGUE Leader, you can take control over your own professional development destiny.

I'm glad to have some willing coconspirators who are ready to change professional development along with me.

Thank you for taking this journey with me.

It's time, once again.

ROGUE Leaders unite.

The journey isn't over. It's only just beginning.

Now is the time.

Be the ROGUE Leader that you were meant to be.

Go forth and go ROGUE!

PD Rules in Review:

1 ***Always meet with a purpose***. Focus on why you are meeting in the first place. Be intentional. Meet with your purpose in mind. Share that purpose with everyone involved. Let others know why you are gathering and give them a reason for being there.

2 ***Be consistent***. Make PD a regular part of the routine. Find a consistent time each week or month that can be dedicated to professional learning. Don't skip out on opportunities to grow and learn.

3 ***Get involved***. Don't sit idly by and let PD be done to you. Work from the inside to make it better. Don't just complain about bad PD. Take action to improve professional development. You are ultimately in charge of your own PD destiny.

4 ***Bring your passion***. PD works better when you are passionate about what you are learning about. Passion can be contagious. Ideas will spread. Others will learn. They will in turn become passionate about their own learning.

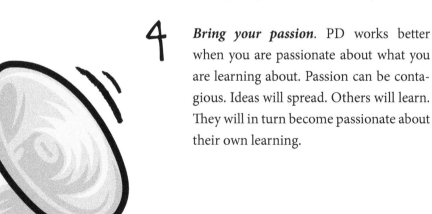

5   *Find others willing to join your pursuit.* Become a recruiter. Find others who are also tired of problematic PD. Convince them that you can tackle the problem together. Build a small army of the willing.

6   *Look for the obvious.* Find the glaring needs. Look for pain points. Keep your ears to the ground and listen for areas of dissatisfaction. Deliver on the obvious needs.

7   *Address wants and needs (and everything in between)!* Create PD that addresses areas that colleagues excel at. Address areas in which teachers need help. Pinpoint topics on which teachers want help. Find a way to focus on the whole learner!

8   *Time is precious—don't waste it.* Don't waste your own time with bad PD. Don't waste someone else's time with bad PD. Always start and end on time. Never use more time than you actually need.

9   *There's no such thing as bad (self-initiated) PD.* If you take PD into your own hands, you will learn something. You know what you need. You know what's going to help. You know how you should be spending your time. Take responsibility for your own PD.

10   *When in doubt, if a rule is not working, break it, or make your own rule.* Do what you want to improve PD. Do what you can to make it better. No matter what. Don't accept no for answer. Break the rules if you must, or make them up as you go.

References

Carver-Thomas, Desiree, and Linda Darling-Hammond. "Teacher Turnover: Why It Matters and What We Can Do About It." Palo Alto, CA: Learning Policy Institute, 2017. https://learningpolicyinstitute.org/sites/default/files/product-files/Teacher_Turnover_REPORT.pdf.

"KISS (Keep It Simple, Stupid)—a Design Principle." The Interaction Design Foundation. Accessed March 26, 2021. https://www.interaction-design.org/literature/article/kiss-keep-it-simple-stupid-a-design-principle.

"The First E-mail Message of Ray Tomlinson." History Computer. Accessed March 26, 2021. https://history-computer.com/the-first-e-mail-message-of-ray-tomlinson.

Acknowledgments

Thank you, first and foremost, to my family for all of your love and support through the years. Thank you for giving me the chance to write and pursue this passion.

Thank you to all of the educators who inspired, collaborated, and shared by going ROGUE and pushing the boundaries in professional development: Max Achtau, Meredith Akers, Brian Aspinall, Nili Bartley, Jay Billy, Starsha Canaday, Tony Cattani, Chris Corney-McGee, Jon Craig, Dr. Michael Curran, Chris Dodge, Mandy Ellis, Cara Flodmand, Mark French, Jennifer Gonzalez, Susan Kotch, Brian Kulak, Adam Lindstrom, Tara Martin, James Moffett, Jim O'Boyle, Glenn Robbins, Stacy Saia, John Spencer, James Sterenczak, Amy Storer, Brittany Tirro, and Joe Valver.

Thank you to the #4OCFPLN, the greatest book club there was! You continue to model what it means to go ROGUE each and every day. Thank you for changing professional learning for yourself and others.

Thank you to those colleagues who have continued to help me grow as a person and as a professional at every step of the way: Jen Braverman, Mike Bryce, Cindy Cooney, Alex Handzus, Shaun Laurito, Kyle Perrine, and Liz Thomas.

Thank you to the TR Family who inspired me to be a better educator and are always a part of my heart!

Thank you to the entire YES Family! You constantly push me to be a better educator. I am blessed to work with such amazing colleagues each day!

Thank you to Trevor Bryan, my coconspirator and co-founder of Four O'Clock Faculty. Almost twenty years later, I still value and appreciate our conversations and collaboration, and your commitment to making things better!

About the Author

Rich Czyz started his career as a fifth-grade teacher and has served as a basic skills teacher, an instructional coach, an elementary supervisor, and a director of curriculum and instruction. Rich pushed boundaries in each of his roles, implementing new technology and finding better ways to do things. He learned that sometimes

challenging the status quo is really the only way to go. Rich is currently the proud principal of the Yardville Elementary School in New Jersey, where he loves to show students what Wiffle ball is all about.

Rich is the cofounder of *The Four O'Clock Faculty* blog for educators looking to improve instruction and learning for themselves and their students. Rich is also the author of *The Four O'Clock Faculty: A ROGUE Guide to Revolutionizing Professional Development* and *The Secret Sauce: Essential Ingredients for Exceptional Teaching*. Rich is passionate about engaging all stakeholders in meaningful and relevant learning opportunities. He is an author, a blogger, and a presenter.

Learn more about Rich by following him on Twitter at @RACzyz or visiting fouroclockfaculty.com.

Bring Rich to Your Next School or District Professional Development Event

Rich Czyz is available for consulting opportunities, speaking engagements, presentations, professional development sessions, speeches, and keynote addresses on a wide range of relevant education topics. He specializes in the following topics:

- Getting Started as a New Teacher
- Personalized Professional Development
- Student Engagement Strategies
- Integrating Technology Across the Curriculum
- Educational Leadership
- Positive School Climate and Culture
- Student Ownership, Voice, and Choice
- Using Data to Guide Instruction
- Productivity for Educators

Please contact Rich via email at 4oclockfaculty@gmail.com to learn more about consulting and speaking opportunities.

Find exclusive chapter resources and more
ROGUE Leader information here:

fouroclockfaculty.com/rogueleader

More from

Dave Burgess Consulting, Inc.

Since 2012, DBCI has published books that inspire and equip educators to be their best. For more information on our titles or to purchase bulk orders for your school, district, or book study, visit DaveBurgessConsulting.com/DBCIbooks.

More from the *Like a PIRATE*™ Series

Teach Like a PIRATE by Dave Burgess

eXPlore Like a PIRATE by Michael Matera

Learn Like a PIRATE by Paul Solarz

Plan Like a PIRATE by Dawn M. Harris

Play Like a PIRATE by Quinn Rollins

Run Like a PIRATE by Adam Welcome

Tech Like a PIRATE by Matt Miller

Lead Like a PIRATE™ Series

Lead Like a PIRATE by Shelley Burgess and Beth Houf

Balance Like a PIRATE by Jessica Cabeen, Jessica Johnson, and Sarah Johnson

Lead beyond Your Title by Nili Bartley

Lead with Appreciation by Amber Teamann and Melinda Miller

Lead with Culture by Jay Billy

Lead with Instructional Rounds by Vicki Wilson

Lead with Literacy by Mandy Ellis

She Leads by Dr. Rachael George and Majalise W. Tolan

Leadership & School Culture

Beyond the Surface of Restorative Practices by Marisol Rerucha

Choosing to See by Pamela Seda and Kyndall Brown

Culturize by Jimmy Casas

Discipline Win by Andy Jacks

Escaping the School Leader's Dunk Tank by Rebecca Coda and Rick Jetter

Fight Song by Kim Bearden

From Teacher to Leader by Starr Sackstein

If the Dance Floor Is Empty, Change the Song by Joe Clark

The Innovator's Mindset by George Couros

It's OK to Say "They" by Christy Whittlesey

Kids Deserve It! by Todd Nesloney and Adam Welcome

Let Them Speak by Rebecca Coda and Rick Jetter

The Limitless School by Abe Hege and Adam Dovico

Live Your Excellence by Jimmy Casas

Next-Level Teaching by Jonathan Alsheimer

The Pepper Effect by Sean Gaillard

Principaled by Kate Barker, Kourtney Ferrua, and Rachael George

The Principled Principal by Jeffrey Zoul and Anthony McConnell

Relentless by Hamish Brewer

The Secret Solution by Todd Whitaker, Sam Miller, and Ryan Donlan

Start. Right. Now. by Todd Whitaker, Jeffrey Zoul, and Jimmy Casas

Stop. Right. Now. by Jimmy Casas and Jeffrey Zoul

Teachers Deserve It by Rae Hughart and Adam Welcome

Teach Your Class Off by CJ Reynolds

They Call Me "Mr. De" by Frank DeAngelis

Thrive through the Five by Jill M. Siler

Unmapped Potential by Julie Hasson and Missy Lennard

When Kids Lead by Todd Nesloney and Adam Dovico

Word Shift by Joy Kirr

Your School Rocks by Ryan McLane and Eric Lowe

Technology & Tools

50 Things to Go Further with Google Classroom by Alice Keeler and Libbi Miller

50 Things You Can Do with Google Classroom by Alice Keeler and Libbi Miller

140 Twitter Tips for Educators by Brad Currie, Billy Krakower, and Scott Rocco

Block Breaker by Brian Aspinall

Building Blocks for Tiny Techies by Jamila "Mia" Leonard

Code Breaker by Brian Aspinall

The Complete EdTech Coach by Katherine Goyette and Adam Juarez

Control Alt Achieve by Eric Curts

The Esports Education Playbook by Chris Aviles, Steve Isaacs, Christine Lion-Bailey, and Jesse Lubinsky

Google Apps for Littles by Christine Pinto and Alice Keeler

Master the Media by Julie Smith

Raising Digital Leaders by Jennifer Casa-Todd

Reality Bytes by Christine Lion-Bailey, Jesse Lubinsky, and Micah Shippee, PhD

Sail the 7 Cs with Microsoft Education by Becky Keene and Kathi Kersznowski

Shake Up Learning by Kasey Bell

Social LEADia by Jennifer Casa-Todd

Stepping Up to Google Classroom by Alice Keeler and Kimberly Mattina

Teaching Math with Google Apps by Alice Keeler and Diana Herrington

Teachingland by Amanda Fox and Mary Ellen Weeks

Teaching with Google Jamboard by Alice Keeler and Kimberly Mattina

Teaching Methods & Materials

All 4s and 5s by Andrew Sharos

Boredom Busters by Katie Powell

The Classroom Chef by John Stevens and Matt Vaudrey

The Collaborative Classroom by Trevor Muir

Copyrighteous by Diana Gill

CREATE by Bethany J. Petty

Ditch That Homework by Matt Miller and Alice Keeler

Ditch That Textbook by Matt Miller

Don't Ditch That Tech by Matt Miller, Nate Ridgway, and
    Angelia Ridgway

EDrenaline Rush by John Meehan

Educated by Design by Michael Cohen, The Tech Rabbi

The EduProtocol Field Guide by Marlena Hebern and
    Jon Corippo

The EduProtocol Field Guide: Book 2 by Marlena Hebern and
    Jon Corippo

The EduProtocol Field Guide: Math Edition by Lisa Nowakowski
    and Jeremiah Ruesch

Expedition Science by Becky Schnekser

Frustration Busters by Katie Powell

Fully Engaged by Michael Matera and John Meehan

Game On? Brain On! by Lindsay Portnoy, PhD

Guided Math AMPED by Reagan Tunstall

Innovating Play by Jessica LaBar-Twomy and Christine Pinto

Instant Relevance by Denis Sheeran

Keeping the Wonder by Jenna Copper, Ashley Bible,
    Abby Gross, and Staci Lamb

LAUNCH by John Spencer and A.J. Juliani

Make Learning MAGICAL by Tisha Richmond

Pass the Baton by Kathryn Finch and Theresa Hoover

Project-Based Learning Anywhere by Lori Elliott

Pure Genius by Don Wettrick

The Revolution by Darren Ellwein and Derek McCoy

Shift This! by Joy Kirr

Skyrocket Your Teacher Coaching by Michael Cary Sonbert

Spark Learning by Ramsey Musallam

Sparks in the Dark by Travis Crowder and Todd Nesloney

Table Talk Math by John Stevens

Unpack Your Impact by Naomi O'Brien and LaNesha Tabb

The Wild Card by Hope and Wade King

The Writing on the Classroom Wall by Steve Wyborney

You Are Poetry by Mike Johnston

Inspiration, Professional Growth & Personal Development

Be REAL by Tara Martin

Be the One for Kids by Ryan Sheehy

The Coach ADVenture by Amy Illingworth

Creatively Productive by Lisa Johnson

Educational Eye Exam by Alicia Ray

The EduNinja Mindset by Jennifer Burdis

Empower Our Girls by Lynmara Colón and Adam Welcome

Finding Lifelines by Andrew Grieve and Andrew Sharos

The Four O'Clock Faculty by Rich Czyz

How Much Water Do We Have? by Pete and Kris Nunweiler

P Is for Pirate by Dave and Shelley Burgess

A Passion for Kindness by Tamara Letter

The Path to Serendipity by Allyson Apsey

Sanctuaries by Dan Tricarico

Saving Sycamore by Molly B. Hudgens

The SECRET SAUCE by Rich Czyz

Shattering the Perfect Teacher Myth by Aaron Hogan

Stories from Webb by Todd Nesloney

Talk to Me by Kim Bearden

Teach Better by Chad Ostrowski, Tiffany Ott, Rae Hughart, and Jeff Gargas

Teach Me, Teacher by Jacob Chastain

Teach, Play, Learn! by Adam Peterson

The Teachers of Oz by Herbie Raad and Nathan Lang-Raad

TeamMakers by Laura Robb and Evan Robb

Through the Lens of Serendipity by Allyson Apsey

The Zen Teacher by Dan Tricarico

Children's Books

Beyond Us by Aaron Polansky

Cannonball In by Tara Martin

Dolphins in Trees by Aaron Polansky

I Can Achieve Anything by MoNique Waters

I Want to Be a Lot by Ashley Savage

The Princes of Serendip by Allyson Apsey

Ride with Emilio by Richard Nares

The Wild Card Kids by Hope and Wade King

Zom-Be a Design Thinker by Amanda Fox

CPSIA information can be obtained
at www.ICGtesting.com
Printed in the USA
BVHW091355130222
628734BV00003B/9